Managing Complexity of Information Systems

Managing Complexity
of
Information Systems

The value of simplicity

Pirmin Lemberger
Médéric Morel

First published 2012 in Great Britain and the United States by ISTE Ltd and John Wiley & Sons, Inc.

ISTE Ltd
27-37 St George's Road
London SW19 4EU
UK

www.iste.co.uk

John Wiley & Sons, Inc.
111 River Street
Hoboken, NJ 07030
USA

www.wiley.com

© ISTE Ltd 2012

The rights of Pirmin Lemberger and Médéric Morel to be identified as the author of this work have been asserted by them in accordance with the Copyright, Designs and Patents Act 1988.

Library of Congress Cataloging-in-Publication Data

Lemberger, Pirmin.
  Managing complexity of information systems : the value of simplicity (TBC) / Pirmin Lemberger, Médéric Morel.
p. cm.
Includes bibliographical references and index.
  ISBN 978-1-84821-341-8
  1. Management information systems. 2. Technological complexity. 3. Information technology. I. Morel, Médéric. II. Title.
  T58.6.L447 2011
  658.4'038011--dc23
                                                                                        2011042577

British Library Cataloguing-in-Publication Data
A CIP record for this book is available from the British Library
ISBN: 978-1-84821-341-8

Printed and bound in Great Britain by CPI Group (UK) Ltd., Croydon, Surrey CR0 4YY

Table of Contents

Foreword

"Science does not think!"

In this famous and controversial statement[1], the philosopher Martin Heidegger certainly did not mean that scientists were stupid or that science was irrational. He was rather expressing the fact that science did not take time to think about itself, meaning its own goals and practices. This can inevitably lead to excesses or undesired results.

The book you are holding could be entitled "IT doesn't think", or "IT does not think enough!" Starting from scratch, it rethinks the goals of a "good" information system, asking what a "good" information system is, beyond choosing the "best" technology and beyond meeting deadlines or budget constraints.

The answer proposed here, "simplicity of the IS", relies on a thorough analysis of the countless sources of complexity that tend to make the IS into a chaotic jumble, which is hard to maintain and even more difficult to improve. This situation penalizes companies striving to remain viable in a fast-moving and competitive environment.

---

1 *What is called thinking?*, Martin Heidegger, Harper Perennial, 1976.

The value of this book is not in this or that specific recommendation but rather in the global vision that justifies the recommendations that are being made.

One of the major insights of this book is its repeated emphasis on the human factor, whether from the point of view of end-users or that of IT Departments.

IT people are often considered introverts who are uninterested in anything other than the latest techno hype. Because they also generally have a hard time meeting deadlines and budgets restrictions, IT management inundates them with technological, architectural, and organizational dictates. The necessity to master this vast array of tools, languages, and methods can leave them feeling disempowered.

The authors of this book argue that one should trust those on the frontlines and that some freedom should be given back to them, because the authors believe that this is the only way to build an IS with a minimum of common sense, which is to say, by never losing sight of the idea that simplicity, the essence of an IS, is not a goal but an ongoing journey.

It is not possible, unfortunately, to drop everything and start over from scratch: our hope is thus to determine where we want to go, to map out our journey, to regularly check that we are not straying from the chosen path, while giving ourselves the leeway to gaze at the panoramas before us and perhaps choose yet another path.

This book should be considered a sort of "survival guide", simple enough to be usable and thorough enough to be relevant.

Pascal Grojean
Managing Director, Emoxa
Co-author of the books *SOA Architect's Guide and Performance of IT Architectures.*

Preface

Many organizations are now reaching the same conclusion: mastering technical and organizational complexity is today the primary difficulty to overcome for their IT departments, much more so than reaching some critical magnitude in IT investments. At best, poorly managed complexity will prevent any reliable predictions for possible future evolutions of the system. At worst, the sustainability of the system as a whole could be put at stake. It would obviously be illusory, if not naive, to attempt to remove complexity altogether from the IS. The aim is rather to master the growth of complexity and to make sure that it stays in reasonable proportion to the actual usefulness of the IS to its various stakeholders. More precisely, the goal is to avoid an uncontrolled proliferation of "useless" complexity to ensure the scalability of the system and to maintain the satisfaction of its users.

This book develops the point of view according to which mastering complexity implies two essential steps: first, we must develop a *clear understanding* of the real nature of complexity within the IS; second, we must *identify the primary causes*, which contribute to its uncontrolled growth and organize these into a logical framework, in order to define efficient countermeasures. We also consider that any serious explanation for IT complexity should deal with both technical and psychological causes of complexity.

Two themes make up the main thread of our book: complexity and value. Both themes are quite common when considered separately. Their interplay, however, has remained a largely unexplored topic.

Our approach to IS complexity combines theoretical analysis with practical field experience. This kind of comprehensive analysis differs, we believe, from both academic works, which focus mostly on theoretical computing and also from so-called pragmatic approaches that simply list catalogs of recipes without bothering to provide a sound conceptual basis for them.

Target audience

This book will be of interest to CIOs as well as to enterprise architects and project managers. Parts of it are written on a more conceptual level than most IT books. This will perhaps require some readers to postpone somewhat their legitimate desire to rush out and apply simplicity rules to real life. We believe, however, that this postponement is worthwhile and the reader will be rewarded with a deeper, and thus more efficient, understanding of the true origins of unmanageable complexity in the IS.

Acknowledgments

This book would not have been possible without the support of SQLI CEO Julien Mériaudeau.

The authors would like especially to express their gratitude to several colleagues, who kindly agreed to share their expert knowledge and experience. Special thanks go to: Mr. Manuel Alves, director of Alcyonix Paris, an Enterprise Architect whose extensive experience in software engineering and project management, and sharp critical mind proved invaluable when it came to confronting theoretical analysis with practical IT issues.

Mr. Simon-Pierre Nolin, senior consultant in IT infrastructure at Alcyonix, provided his deep insights and extensive field experience regarding how simplicity principles could be implemented in IT operations.

The authors thank Dr. Julian Talbot from the Laboratory of Theoretical Physics of Condensed Matter at Pierre et Marie Curie University in Paris for his critical proofreading of an early version of the manuscript.

The authors thank especially Mr. Jean-Luc Raffaëlli, Strategic Project Director at Groupe La Poste and Mr. Pierre Bonnet co-founder of Orchestra Networks for their insights and feedbacks.

Last but not least, Mr. J. Patterson Waltz, consultant in processes improvement at Alcyonix, reviewed the whole manuscript with an impressive dedication and thoroughness. Obviously, any remaining inaccuracies or typos remain the sole responsibility of the authors.

Chapter 1

Why Simplicity?

Simplicity is the ultimate sophistication
Leonardo da Vinci

1.1. Solving conflicting requirements

Information systems (ISs) are now ubiquitous in nearly all large companies and organizations. They provide a permanently available online store to customers. They automate an ever-increasing proportion of business processes and tasks, thus contributing to the rationalization effort and cost reduction required by the globalization of competition. Senior executives use ISs to perform business activity monitoring that allows them to react quickly in fast-moving markets, where reducing the time to market is more important than ever. ISs have thus truly become an essential tool for sound decision-making as well as for selling or providing goods and services.

We might naively think that such a strategic position would logically call for putting maximal effort into designing robust and perennial systems. However, as most likely any reader of this book will know by experience, such is hardly ever the case. Unlike road networks or buildings, most ISs are not really built or designed to last. Rather, they grow much more like living organisms, responding to a set of fluctuating and contradictory forces while trying to adapt in an open environment. A common situation is one in which the number of users grows, both inside (employees and IT personnel) and outside (customers) the company, while at the same time those same users all become more demanding. They expect more speed, more reliability, more flexibility, and a better user experience and all of these simultaneously.

The most acute conflict between these expectations is probably less between speed and reliability than between flexibility and reliability. Speed could certainly be achieved, at least in principle, by using mere brute force, which means by allotting sufficient technological and human resources to designing and operating the IS. Flexibility, on the other hand, could probably not be achieved even if we had an infinite amount of resources available. The fact that brute force will not do is a hint that what we are facing here is a deeper issue than achieving mere performance. More flexibility typically involves meeting unclear and fluctuating user requirements. Often it also means providing improved customization to all stakeholders. Agility and fast turnaround are thus the key requirements here. Building reliability, on the other hand, requires a lengthy design phase, deep understanding of the interdependence of subsystems, performing many tests, and gathering extensive feedback about the system's behavior. Building reliability means building human understanding, which is in essence a slow process.

At least two other factors often contribute to make the situation even worse. First, there is the successive technological hype for such things as "EAI", "SOA", "EJB",

"MDM", or any other acronym you might have heard floating around in recent years. This succession of technologies will progressively generate uncontrolled complexity in the IS. Second, under such difficult circumstances, some key employees with technical or business skills might simply want to quit and look for a better working environment. Now, sum up all the previously mentioned forces that shape an IS: the need for flexibility, the multifaceted techno-hype, and perhaps a high turnover, and this will quite soon result in an organizational and technological nightmare that is probably best described as chaos! As physicists tell us, chaos is a situation which is unpredictable. This is the exact opposite of why the IS was built in the first place. In such near-chaotic situations, nobody has a clear picture of what the system is really doing, what the information feeds contain, how the data are structured, and which hardware processes are running. Not surprisingly either, nobody wants to assume the responsibility for making any decisions or changes. Incidentally, it is not by chance that most system architecture endeavors start by mapping the existing system because nobody really knows what the system is made of! Does this sound familiar?

This apparently uncontrollable increase in entropy of computing systems is by no means new. The recent need for opening older systems to the web and the plethora of technologies that pretend to be optimal in this respect only exacerbated the existing tendency for computing systems to grow out of control. For nearly half a century, however, software languages, architecture principles, and development processes have been designed to solve this apparent contradiction of building computing systems that are both maintainable, meaning well-structured and understandable by human minds, and, at the same time, flexible enough to accommodate changing requirements. Let us briefly review some of these here.

On the software engineering side, object-oriented programming (OOP) was probably one of the most significant such attempts. In non-technical terms, what OOP in principle does is to allow constructing a larger system from smaller ones by progressive and controlled aggregation. Traditional procedural languages were notoriously bad at achieving such a goal and OOP was, no doubt, a major breakthrough.

Architectural principles were also proposed, with the aim of organizing and decoupling as much as possible the various processing layers. They all involve the idea of using components, which are reusable pieces of software that should be as autonomous and decoupled from the others as possible. The best known example here is probably the three-tier architecture where components in charge of the presentation logic are clearly separated from those in charge of implementing the business rules, which are in turn decoupled from those responsible for recording the data in permanent storage.

More recently, we saw the advent of the so-called service-oriented architecture (SOA), motivated by the need for business-process flexibility and reusing legacy components. SOA proposes a component architecture, not just in terms of the software architecture for one application, but for the whole IS.

Finally, iterative engineering processes were designed, such as *extreme programming* or *Lean Software Development*, to provide controlled methods for dealing with unclear and quickly changing user requirements.

Each of these topics will be treated in depth in later chapters. For now, let us note that this continuous struggle explains why, during the early years of ISs, management was mostly driven by technological innovation. This is the first topic of the following section where we take some time to review the recent history of IS management. The aim will be to put our approach, simplistically , in perspective as the next natural step.

1.2. Three periods in IS management

We can roughly identify three successive periods in IS management. To make our points as clearly as possible, we choose to characterize each era, the reality being obviously less clear-cut.

1.2.1. *Management driven by technology*

Roughly speaking, this period spanned the years from 1970 to 2000. During this time, it was hoped that technological innovation alone would solve the entropy problem and allow building efficient and durable systems. This was the era of monolithic and closed systems where the same vendor would often provide both the software and the hardware running it. IBM and Digital were certainly key players here. Judging by the number of COBOL and UNIX systems still running strategic applications in today's banking systems, we can conclude that this approach had some serious success. This fact should certainly not be neglected and it could probably inspire current technological choices when it comes to thinking in terms of sustainability. We will come back to this later.

Relying on technology alone to drive the evolution of an IS presents two dangers that we refer to as the "fashion victim syndrome" and the "vendor trapping syndrome".

Technological fashion victims trust in technology so blindly that they tend to systematically own the latest gadgets, thinking their life will change forever and for the better. Similar behavior could be observed from some tech-gurus in many IT departments during this first period.

This undoubtedly fueled the impression, an often justified one, that ISs are like black holes, swallowing more and more resources while not producing much more than the previous versions and sometimes even less. As is now apparent to any observant CIO, choosing the latest technologies implies risks that often outweigh the benefits of the hypothetical improvements claimed by the latest hype. This matter of fact led a prominent IT thinker [CAR 03] to make the provocative suggestion that wisdom in this field systematically belong to technology followers rather than to the leaders.

Vendor trapping, on the other hand, is the situation in which the vendor leverages the strong software–hardware coupling to discourage customers from trying competitor's products. The most extreme form of trapping was simply locking: the software could not even run on alternative hardware.

With multi-platform languages like Java having been around for nearly 15 years now, cost-free hardware-agnostic system software like Linux for nearly 20 years, and the openness of IT systems promoted to a quasi-religion, this could sound almost like prehistory. But caution is still needed because the "trapping devil" is certainly not dead yet. Indeed, it has been rather active lately, tempting some of the major IT actors.

1.2.2. *Management through cost reduction*

Largely as a reaction to this first era of IT extravagance, the turn of the century saw the advent of a much more austere era of systematic cost reductions. All of a sudden, ISs came under suspicion. They were perceived as ivory towers hiding a bunch of tech-gurus whose main preoccupation was to play with the latest technologies. Hence the tight control on spending, where each dollar had to be justified by immediate and measurable gains in business productivity.

This cost-killing obsession, the fear of the vendor trap, and the advent of the web as a major selling platform were factors that all pushed IT management to favor more open architectures. These architectures were meant to leverage the legacy systems by wrapping functionality of existing systems into reusable services to open the old platforms to the web where the business was progressively shifting.

This was, and still is, the Java–Linux area. The Java language, with its motto "write once, run everywhere", was, at least apparently, the way to go for avoiding the vendor trap. The Linux operating system, on the other hand, was to contribute to cost reduction by avoiding the prohibitive license costs that would result when the IS needs to rescale.

One important consequence of IT management teams driven primarily by cost reduction was that overdesigning and modeling an IS were considered a luxury one could no longer afford. Consequently, any form of abstract thinking was deemed academic and nearly useless. "Keep it Simple Stupid" was the new motto. That probably also favored the advent of off-the-shelf solutions in the form of ERP[1] packages. Explicit coding was to be replaced by mere customization. SAP and Oracle are likely the most prominent players in this ERP category.

Pushing outsourcing to its limits was still another consequence of the cost-cutting struggle. The outsourcing of specialized IT skills certainly began way before the cost reduction era; however, it is during this era that off-shore development really took off. It was motivated solely by the availability of a cheaper labor force in emergent countries for low value-added tasks such as coding specified software components. Experience showed, however, that the expected

---

[1] *Enterprise Resource Planning* refers to an integrated application used to manage internal and external resources, including tangible assets, financial resources, materials, and human resources.

cost savings did not always materialize because the effort incurred by additional coordination and specification was often underestimated.

As an increasing number of IT departments are now starting to realize, this drastic cost reduction period also often led to an accumulation of a heterogeneous set of technologies that were not really mastered. In a sense, many ISs just grew out of control, behaving like a set of cancer cells. Eventually, the initial attempt to reduce costs often resulted in expensive re-engineering processes and in massive system architecture endeavors, which could last for years, with no guarantee of success.

Much was learned, however, from this era. The most important lesson probably being that "cost reduction" alone cannot be the single driving force for building a sustainable and flexible IS.

1.2.3. *Management through value creation*

More recently, other approaches emerged for IT management teams, which by contrast with the previous approach are based on a somewhat more positive concept than "cost reduction", namely that of "value creation". In this perspective, the IS is considered an important intangible asset of a company that provides a substantial competitive advantage in a similar way as ordinary know-how, R&D, or copyrights do. A possible definition of the IS from this perspective could actually be the following: "The IS contains, or more simply is, the explicit knowledge of an organization".

As for any other intangible asset, the contribution of the IS to value generation is not only hard to measure, but, more significantly, also difficult to define properly on a purely conceptual level. This difficulty can be traced back to a set of features of ISs that distinguish them from other assets:

– ISs are typically very complicated systems that grew slowly over time without the actual possibility to ever measure the exact amount of effort that went into their design, construction, and maintenance. As mentioned before, ISs grow more like living organisms because of their complexity and openness.

– When considering generation of value, it becomes very hard, if not impossible, to clearly disentangle the contribution of the IS seen as a technical tool from other contributions such as the knowledge and the skills of the IT people in charge of its maintenance and development. The efficiency of the processes in the organization in which the IS operates obviously plays a big role regarding the generation of value. Indeed, even a technically robust IS could collapse within just a few months if key skilled personnel leave or if the same inappropriate changes are made to core processes in the IT department.

– Most often, ISs are unique systems, crafted for one company to answer its specific needs. Therefore, there is no real IS market that could help define a price or a value of an IS. Putting things differently, ISs are not easy to compare for the simple reason that they are intrinsically unique.

– Another rarely mentioned but fundamental difficulty in assessing the value of an IS is what we might call the present-or-future ambiguity. What if an IS, which is currently doing a perfect job as a generator of value, had only limited flexibility to accommodate future opportunities? Most IT managers and CIOs would certainly agree that this IS has poor value. Any sensible concept of value for an IS should thus take into account not just the current situation, but also its sustainability.

Yet, this confused situation has not discouraged many IT thinkers from talking, writing, and commenting endlessly about IS value. As is usual in such circumstances, the conceptual mess is never really eliminated but is rather recycled by those who see an opportunity to invent a plethora of theories to help them sell their precious experience and expertise.

That being said, it should be acknowledged that some of these approaches are of interest and could even have practical use. A common idea is to try and quantify an appropriate concept of *Use Value*, a concept that actually goes back as far as Marx's major work, *Capital*. No doubt it is interesting to try to apply this concept to IS, even if it is only to see its limits. As the original definition by Marx was intrinsically subjective, the first task for any "use value theorist" will be to try and quantify it for the specific case of an IS. We shall come back to this in more detail in Chapter 3.

The advantage of these kinds of value-driven approaches to IS management is that they are based on actual measurements, which are certainly reassuring for the IT management teams who choose to use them. Their main weakness, however, lies in the great deal of arbitrariness they involve, both in what is measured and in how it is measured. As a quick example, many of these approaches neglect sustainability aspects of the IS altogether.

Thus, once more, this third era of the IT management has undoubtedly brought us a few steps closer to wiser and more lucid IT management. Quite clearly, however, use value cannot be the whole story either.

1.3. And now ... simplicity!

1.3.1. *Technology, cost reduction, value creation ... So what's next?*

On the one hand, the idea of maximizing some sort of use value that emerged from the last management era looks to be on the right track. But at the same time, it really sounds too simplistic. Any CIO or IT professional in charge of a large IS could probably easily come up with real-life examples where use value is not the only thing worth considering. We previously mentioned sustainability, but even that would leave out many other important facets of the usefulness of an IS.

So, let us just face it: no single concept of value will ever suffice to capture what the desirable state is for an IS, both at present and in the future. In no way can this "set of desirable features" for an IS be summarized in just one number, even with a very sophisticated concept of value. Attempting to summarize a quantity which is in essence a multi-component quantity into a single-component quantity is just wrong and can only mislead those who are in charge of making decisions. For these reasons, we believe that use value alone cannot provide safe guidance for IS management in the long run.

Once this weakness of any single-component concept of IS value has been acknowledged, one first and obvious step could be to define, more appropriately, a set of several, well-justified, concepts of values. Certainly, these should be both relevant and reasonably independent from one another. Chapter 3 follows this line of thought. But clearly, to be content with a move from a scalar concept of value to a mere set of values would expose our approach to the very same criticism that we made in the first place against the "use value", namely that of arbitrariness. And this certainly would be a legitimate criticism.

Is there any way out? We believe there is! There is a deeper concept behind this set of desirable features that an IS should possess. This concept we believe is, well, simplicity! Behind this deceptively obvious, intuitive and apparently provocative word "simplicity" lies a rich, deep, and multifaceted set of concepts that we think could provide the much-sought guidance for the state and evolution of an IS.

> The aim of this book is to make these concepts of simplicity precise and operational in real IT life. Our line of thought is that a proper conceptual understanding of simplicity is a prerequisite for sound decision making in IT.

As it happens, the complexity of IS, which in a very rough sense (too rough indeed as we shall see later) could be considered the counterpart of simplicity, has come under close scrutiny of much academic and applied research in recent years. We shall briefly review a selection of these results in Chapter 2, namely those we consider the most relevant for our subject. Although not devoid of interest, many of these works about complexity of IS somehow implement the same strategy as that of previously mentioned works on the value of an IS. It is usually argued that one single concept of complexity, taken from software engineering or from graph theory, could be miraculously appropriate for measuring the complexity of an IS, provided it is suitably generalized or enhanced. In other words, existing concepts of complexity are used and applied explicitly, as is, to ISs.

Again, we think this approach is, by far, too simplistic and will not in fact be able to reliably describe the reality of an IS, where human, organizational, and technological complexities are inextricably entangled. Neither will a contrived concept of use value or complexity do. We need more. We need some form of practical wisdom for IS management.

1.4. Plan of the book

To build this wisdom, our strategy will not be to start from scratch and concoct some entirely new concepts of simplicity and complexity. Rather, we will draw on various areas of research that have resulted in an in-depth understanding of complexity and simplicity. This is the content of Chapter 2.

– The first of these domains is *information theory*, which is a part of mathematics. For more than half a century, mathematicians have struggled to understand complexity and related concepts such as information and randomness. They tried to do so by removing as much as possible any kind of arbitrariness. No doubt this is certainly a good place to go for those who look for complexity concepts that are robust and deep. However, the conclusion of this quick tour will not be an easy set of ready-to-use recipes for measuring the complexity of an IS. But it will be a deeper conceptual understanding of what complexity is, in a restricted framework where it can be defined rigorously.

– The second topic we will draw from is *design*. In a beautiful and famous little book [MAE 06], John Maeda from MIT proposed a designer's look at simplicity for which he proposed 10 laws. These are not mere negations or antitheses of the complexity concepts suggested by the information theory, for at least two reasons. The first and most obvious one is that designers and mathematicians have very different types of concerns. While mathematicians are in quest of intrinsic and robust concepts, designers, on the other hand, take into account human factors that we believe are essential ingredients when dealing with ISs and how humans use them. Second, simplicity is a more positive concept that cannot be simply cast as negative complexity.

– The last topic on which we shall draw is *software engineering*, whose relationship with ISs is rather obvious when compared to the previous perhaps more exotic topics. This more conservative approach has strengths and weaknesses of its own. The strength is that it can provide a set of metrics for various aspects of IT complexities that have already proven their validity for some very specific contexts. The weakness, as we already mentioned, is the rather high level of arbitrariness of the suggested metrics.

There are deep connections between the concepts of complexity and the value, which are actually already implicit in the idealized mathematical concepts, as we shall see. Our task thus will be to bring them out and make them explicit. To that end, in Chapter 3, we shall first select a few relevant concepts of values for an IS. The famous use value will be part of the set. This part can be read as a quick introduction to the most common concept of values used in IT. We shall argue that the concepts we retain are all reasonably independent from one another and equally relevant in most practical situations. This part of the book lays the conceptual foundations for implementing simplicity in IS.

Later, in Chapter 4, we identify how the main sources of uncontrolled complexity can be mitigated using our simplicity principles to increase the value of an IS. This chapter is more practical than the previous chapter.

Rephrasing the above slightly, we can consider that a set of well-chosen concepts of value is basically a *black-box view* of an IS. In no way, however, is it adequate to drive the evolution of an IS. Deeper understanding and more lucidity is needed. Complexity and simplicity enter by providing a *white-box view* of an IS, explaining what the true origin of value is. We stress once more, however, that this understanding does not necessarily lend itself to an easy and ready-to-use set of recipes.

This book is definitely not a for-dummies kind of book. In no way do we claim that simplicity is synonymous with easiness, neither conceptually nor practically. We claim that simplicity is a core value when designing ISs.

For productivity reasons, enterprise computing has often been, and still is, reduced to applying patterns, best practices, and templates at various levels. This is actually closely related to a topic; excessive specialization and the resulting disempowerment, that we shall discuss in depth in Chapter 4. We think this is really a mistake, even with efficiency in mind. ISs naturally raise a number of intrinsically conceptual issues regarding information processing, model building, and evaluating complexity or abstraction. We believe that all these topics deserve, once in a while, a little more conceptual thinking. Chapter 2 has been written in this frame of mind.

Our previous caveats notwithstanding, the book concludes with a purely practical Chapter 5. This chapter actually summarizes several years of our own experience with contracts related to such topics as defining and building modular architectures, performing large-scale business modeling, and designing pivot formats to integrate different systems. We give a number of practical recommendations on how to implement simplicity principles in hardware, software, and functional architecture. We also discuss human and organizational matters in this same layered perspective.

Let us conclude this introduction by acknowledging that some arbitrariness is certainly unavoidable in our approach as well. We believe, however, that it offers improved guidance on how to manage an IS in the long run, when both sustainability and flexibility matter. Simplicity is certainly a more exciting concept than cost reduction. It is also deeper than value creation for which it provides an explanation and suggests practical improvements. Indeed, various aspects of simplicity touch all IS stakeholders: customers, IT managers, and top management. Finally, simplicity has the power of intuitive concepts.

> Rather than trying to optimize one IS value, try to identify the key factors that contribute to different and equally essential concepts of value. This we claim is a CIO's main responsibility!

So, are you ready for a ride through simplicity?

Chapter 2

Complexity, Simplicity, and Abstraction

Recursion is the root of computation since it trades
description for time.
Alan Jay Perlis – Epigrams on Programming

2.1. What does information theory tell us?

We start our journey through complexity and simplicity concepts with mathematics or, more precisely, information theory. This might seem an exotic topic if what we have in mind are applications to the IT world. However, concepts that will be at the core of our future preoccupations, information, randomness, and especially complexity have all been under close scrutiny by mathematicians for over more than half a century now. In their hands, these concepts have evolved into a set of ideas, which is both deep and robust. Moreover, information theory is actually one of those few areas where mathematics succeeded in rigorously formalizing imprecise, almost philosophical concepts, such as complexity and information, to which they bring a unique insight. It would thus seem unreasonable for us to overlook this body of knowledge altogether. These information theory concepts form a collection of metaphors that will help us build a healthy intuition that will prove helpful later when we venture into less rigorous but more practical IT concepts. As we shall see, this first look at the subject, through mathematical glasses, also highlights a number of important issues and limitations, which occur as soon as one seriously attempts to define complexity.

As information theory is a highly technical and abstract topic, we can barely afford here to do more than just scratch the surface. We shall strive to present in plain language the major findings in information theory of relevance to us. The interested reader will find more details in Appendix 1.

Our quick overview of information theory will focus on only three concepts: *Shannon's entropy*, *K-complexity*, and *Bennett's logical depth*. Assume for simplicity's sake that any object or system, whose complexity we wish to define, is described by a binary sequence s such as 001101110... The three concepts mentioned above have one important point in common: they all evaluate the complexity of a system as the quantity of information that its description s contains, assuming that we have a specific goal in mind for s. This goal, as we shall see, is a foreshadowing, in the restricted mathematical context, of the concept of value that we shall examine in Chapter 3. To make things as concrete as possible, we start with an example drawn from classical computing [DEL 99].

Suppose we want to assign a complexity to the compiled code of an algorithm that solves a certain class of problems. The system under consideration here is thus a piece of software. The binary sequence s that describes it is simply the compiled code. The goal we are trying to reach when compiling the source code to create s is something like this:

– First, we would like the compiled code to run as fast as possible. Thus, compiled code that runs fast is certainly of higher value than slower code.

– Also, we would like the compiled code to be as short as possible. A program with a low memory footprint will thus be of high value. The latter condition is in this day and age less important than the first one. Compared to the first criteria, we might thus give it a lower weight in our evaluation of the complexity of s.

– Finally, we can consider that the larger the set of problems the algorithm is able to solve, the higher the value of the compiled code will be.

To this list of quantitative features one could add still other things like the portability of the compiled code or its originality. In any case, the goal is some suitably weighted combination of all these quantitative and qualitative wishes. Altogether, they determine the value of the information or complexity enclosed in the compiled code s. The price at which we would sell the code would probably be strongly correlated to such a goal.

From this simple example, we learn that one good idea could be:

> Define complexity of an object as the value of the information contained in its binary description, assuming a specific goal has been assigned.

For realistic goals such as the goal mentioned in the above example, there is unfortunately no full-fledged mathematical theory available. However, for simpler but still significant goals, there is. We now briefly review the three of greatest relevance to our subject.

2.1.1. *Shannon's entropy*

Historically, the first concept of information to be formulated in mathematically rigorous terms was that of Shannon's[1] entropy. There are many different interpretations to Shannon's entropy. For our purposes and to provide a basis for further reflection, we shall present it first as a measure of the amount or randomness present in a system. Later, we shall briefly explain how this amount of randomness is related to an average quantity of information and also to an idea of complexity.

The idea is probably best understood by recalling the original context in which Shannon formulated his concept. Shannon was looking for an optimal method to compress information to transmit over noisy communication channels (an electric wire or radio waves). For this, he modeled a source of information such as a text to be transmitted, as a random generator of characters. We may indeed think of a large text in a given language, English or French, as being made up of a random sequence of characters whose probabilities are known in advance (the character "e" occurs more often than "k" in English, for instance).

The goal that we referred to in the previous section is here: "Encode strings of characters, whose probabilities are known, in such a way that their average encoded length is as short as possible".

Shannon found an explicit solution to this problem, which we will not examine in detail here. The intuition behind his solution is, however, easy to grasp: it says, in a precise way, that frequently occurring characters should be encoded with short strings. These solutions are described, with minimal

---

1 Claude Elwood Shannon (1916–2001) was an American mathematician, electronic engineer, and cryptographer recognized as "the father of information theory".

mathematical artillery in Appendix 1. However, for the moment, there are only two important things to understand here:

– The average length of encodings in Shannon's solution turns out to be larger if the source is more random (see Appendix 1 for an example). *Shannon's entropy* is, by definition, *the average length of this optimal encoding*. It is thus a genuine measure of randomness of the source of characters.

– The average length of Shannon's optimal solution turns out to be dependent on the probabilities of occurrence of each character only and not on the precise character set or alphabet that is being used. Therefore, Shannon's entropy has a significance that reaches far beyond Shannon's original question on finding optimal encodings. It is in fact a *measure of randomness of any random event whose probabilities are known*.

The *relation of Shannon's entropy to an amount of information* is obtained by rephrasing point 1 a little. When the randomness of a message is weak, we know ahead of time what the outcome will be. In other words, we do not gain much information when we learn the outcome of the random experiment. By contrast, if the source was highly unpredictable we gain a lot of information as soon as we learn the outcome that we could not have guessed in advance.

We postpone the relation of Shannon's entropy with complexity to the following section on Kolmogorov complexity, where it fits more naturally.

One last and very important property of *Shannon's entropy is* that it is *very easy to compute* once we are given the probabilities of the random events. Unfortunately, this ease of computation has led to numerous cases of misuse of

Shannon's entropy, even when no genuine probabilities were available. Although there are few direct applications of this concept to IT; we chose to quickly present it because of its historical significance and because it makes a natural introduction to our next concept.

2.1.2. *Kolmogorov complexity*

In its original formulation, Shannon's entropy, as we have just seen, measures the randomness of a source of information that produces a random output (say strings of characters). But what if we would like to assign a complexity to a single object or system or string of characters? It turns out that there is such a concept. It is called *Kolmogorov[2] complexity* or K-complexity for short.

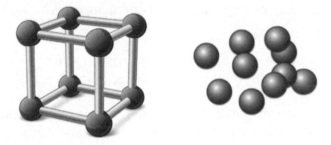

Figure 2.1. *Regular objects, such as crystals, have simple description. They have a highly compressible description and thus have a low K-complexity. The description of a random system, such as a gas of particles, on the other hand, can hardly be compressed and is associated with a high K-complexity. K-complexity is thus a measure of the compressibility of the description of a system*

Its formal definition is somewhat technical, but its essence, as we shall see, is quite simple to understand. K-complexity is one possible measure of the amount of

---

2 Andrey Nikolaevich Kolmogorov (1903–1987) was a Soviet Russian mathematician, who advanced mathematics and logic, including computational complexity.

information contained in a binary string. The binary string could be the description of an object or not. It could be the sequence of characters of this book, a set of UML diagrams, the code of your browser, or the first digits of π. Suppose now that our goal is to compress this binary sequence as much as possible. Finally, we measure the length of this most compact form of the original string. Well this length is, in very rough terms, the K-complexity of the string.

The K-complexity of a binary string is the length of its most compressed form.

As it stands, this intuitive definition immediately raises a number of questions. What exactly do we mean by compressing a binary string? Is there a unique and optimal way to do this? Otherwise, how would this definition make sense at all?

The formal definition of K-complexity requires the introduction of devices known as *Turing machines*. For our purposes, we shall consider them simply as conceptual versions of usual computers. Like ordinary computers, Turing machines run programs and output a result. Both the programs and the output are binary strings. The optimal compressed form of a binary string is nothing other than the shortest program that, when we run it on our Turing machine, gives us back our original string. If the string has a lot of structures in it, for example if there is pattern that repeats periodically like 011011011..., then the program that outputs this string can be much shorter than the original string. On the other hand, when the string is "random" and has no structure in it, then only an explicit output operation can produce our string. No compression is possible. The length of this output-operation program is just slightly over the length of the original string.

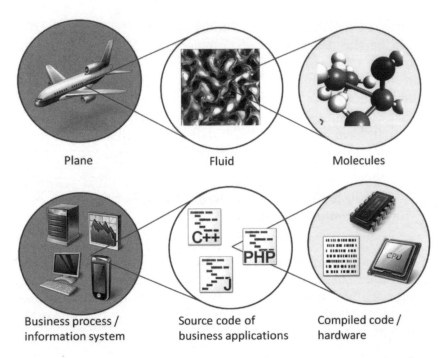

Plane   Fluid   Molecules

Business process /   Source code of   Compiled code /
information system   business applications hardware

Figure 2.2. *Describing the complexity of an object or a system requires first choosing an appropriate scale of description. It is to this description that a K-complexity is associated, not to the system itself. This is true both in classical engineering and in engineering of information systems*

It can be shown (though we will not do it here) that the length of this shortest program does not depend, in a significant way, on the type of Turing machine we chose, at least when considering very long strings. This independence legitimizes K-complexity as an intrinsic measure of complexity. It is at the root of information theory.

2.1.2.1. *Complexity of objects versus complexity of binary strings*

It seems natural to define the K-complexity of an object or of a system as the K-complexity of its description in a binary form. Unfortunately, there is an ambiguity here because most physical objects or systems have various scales of description. Consider a large information system (IS). Describing the IS on a macroscopic level could be achieved in terms of use cases, for instance. On a more fine-grained scale, we could consider the source code of the applications as another valid description. Ultimately, on a microscopic scale, we could consider in principle the binary code running on each chip. Each of these descriptions contains a very different amount of information and thus we must select one to remove the ambiguity.

> While K-complexity is an attribute of a binary string it is not an attribute of a physical object or of a system.

In section 2.1.4, we propose a definition of an abstraction level for the description of a system (think of UML modeling as a concrete example). The scale of description will be part of what characterizes an abstraction level.

2.1.2.2. *Relation to Shannon's entropy*

On the conceptual level, there is a link between Shannon's entropy and K-complexity that we shall not attempt to justify here but will mention as an interesting and profound result in information theory. It is best understood in the original context of a random string generator whose probabilities are known. If we were to ask: "What is the average of the K-complexities of these random strings assuming we use the probabilities of these strings as weights?" The answer is simple: it is (close to) the Shannon's entropy. In other words, Shannon's entropy in fact turns out to be an averaged version of the K-complexity. Disorder and complexity are thus related in precise sense.

2.1.2.3. *Can we compute K-complexity?*

Shannon's entropy is easy to compute. There is indeed a formula, which is given in the appendix. Unfortunately, there is no such explicit formula for K-complexity. K-complexity is important as a central concept. It allows us to speak rigorously about one type of complexity, and by comparing it to other types, it provides further insight. It is, however, of no practical use to evaluate complexity in concrete cases. Information theory proves that there is no, and never will be, any effective way to compute K-complexity. Here, effective means "in a predictable amount of time".

It is important to understand that this impossibility has nothing to do with lack of imagination or progress in technology. It is a conceptual impossibility rooted in the limit of logic itself to obtain answers to some problems in a predictable amount of time.

We could be more modest and seek useful and computable approximations to K-complexity. There indeed exists such approximation but information theory brings us bad news once again: it will forever be impossible to evaluate the quality of such approximations.

Thus, even for such a simple goal as compressing the information as much as possible, we see that:

> Computing a universal measure of complexity is known to be impossible.

The only way out is to abandon the hope of finding a universal and computable concept of complexity and to look for complexity measures that are restricted to certain topics. Such examples will be discussed in section 2.3.1.

2.1.3. *Bennett's logical depth*

Random objects without structure have high K-complexity because, as we discussed, they are not compressible. With ISs in mind, we now realize that K-complexity is perhaps not such a good measure of the kind of complexity we are interested in. What if what we would like is to distinguish *complicated systems*, which are systems that have no short description, from truly *complex systems*, which require a lot of efforts to be produced? The table below summarizes the main differences we can expect between these two forms of complexity.

Complicated objects	Organized objects
Their description is long	Their description could be either long or short
Random objects are always complicated	Random objects are not organized objects
They are easy to produce	They require design or computing to be produced
They can be produced very quickly, and they even occur spontaneously	They grow slowly, and they never occur spontaneously

There is a concept, which formalizes this idea within information theory. It is called Bennett's logical depth. It again fits the scheme where complexity is measured as the amount of information with respect to the goal. For a binary string, this goal would be to "find the description that requires as little computation as possible to reproduce the given string". Bennett's[3] definition can be conveniently formulated in plain language if we use the same tools as for K-complexity. Suppose we have our Turing machine

---

3 Charles H. Bennett is a Fellow at IBM Research. Bennett's recent work has concentrated on applying quantum physics to information exchange. He is one of the founding fathers of quantum information theory.

at hand and we found the shortest possible program p that outputs our string s. Bennett's logical depth is then defined as the number of steps of execution that p needs to produce s.

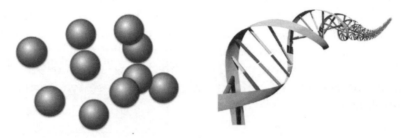

Figure 2.3. *Bennett's logical depth intends to distinguish between organized and unorganized complexity. The random structure on the left has a low logical depth because it does not require much computation or design to be produced. Highly organized systems, such as a strand of DNA or a high-tech device, on the other hand, require a large amount of computation or design to be produced and are logically deep in the sense of Bennett*

Rephrasing the above definition:

> An object has large Bennett logical depth if it encapsulates a great amount of computation or design or results from a long selection process.

Similar remarks apply for K-complexity: Bennett's is as hard to compute and to approximate as K-complexity, unfortunately. When applying the concept to physical systems, a scale of description should be defined beforehand.

To gain some further intuition, let us look at some simple examples from the IT world using the above concepts as metaphors.

	Low K-complexity (short description)	High K-complexity (long description)
Low Bennett depth (no significant design work)	Standard piece of code that is generated automatically. Code for CRUD[4] operations belongs here for instance	Databases with lots of unstructured information
High Bennett depth (significant design work)	Simple business rules (i.e. they are easily described) that need to be coded by hand because they are non-standard (they require significant design effort)	Large and well-structured databases

Large and well-structured code |

Most ISs, taken as a whole, are both Bennett deep and K-complex.

2.1.4. *Abstraction in light of scale and depth*

An interesting by-product of the above discussion on K-complexity and Bennett's depth is that these concepts can help us clarify what is the level of abstraction of the model for a system. This is particularly important, as most complex systems, such as ISs, need several descriptions at different scales. As we will argue later, scale is precisely one of the attributes of an abstraction level of a model.

Having a clear idea of what an abstraction level is will be of particular importance when we discuss abstraction in software engineering in section 2.3.2 and IS modeling best practices in section 4.3.1. Abstraction levels in IT are customarily denoted by well-known terms that correspond, more or less, to layers of IT architecture such as the business process architecture,

---

4 CRUD is the acronym for Create, Read, Update, and Delete, which are the basic data manipulation operations on any set of data.

the software architecture, the application architecture, the hardware architecture, and so on.

To define the level of abstraction of a model of a system, we use an analogy. The system under consideration is represented by a binary string s: think of it as its description at a given scale as we explained earlier. A model of this system, at a given scale, can be considered a compressed version of its explicit description. We thus assimilate a model with a program p that generates the string s through some computing mechanism such as a Turing machine. The Turing machine should be considered here as a metaphor for the design process that leads from the model of a system to the system itself. To set the ideas in an IT context, consider the system as a business application, and its model is a set of UML diagrams.

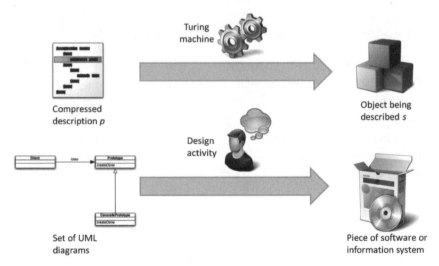

Figure 2.4. *The model for a piece of software can consist of a set of UML diagrams. These diagrams can be thought of as a compressed version of the software to be produced: they are to be read and interpreted by a designer to produce the desired piece of software. This closely parallels the concepts of Bennett's logical depth where a compressed description of an object is a program run by a Turing machine, which produces the explicit description of an object. An abstraction level of the description of a system is characterized, besides the scale, by its level of compression*

What then is a good model? First, the model should be on an appropriate scale. If we want to describe business features of a business application, for instance (corresponding to s), we should model it using a set of UML diagrams that contain only this information and nothing else at a lower scale such as detailed technical information. Second, the model (corresponding to p) should not be too deep in the Bennett sense because this would mean that the amount of design necessary to go from the model to the finished system is very large. However, for models to be useful, they should not require too much additional work to build the system they describe. In other words:

Good models are models at an appropriate scale and for which most of the design effort has gone into the creation of the model. The effort to go from the model to the actual system should be comparatively low.

Thus, the brief discussion given above suggests the following definitions for the abstraction level of a model of a complex system:

– The *scale of description* of a model is the first attribute of an abstraction level.

– The *design effort* needed to go from the model to the real system is the second attribute of an abstraction level.

We will have more to discuss on abstraction in section 2.3.

2.1.5. *Harvesting information theory*

Recall that we have discussed three different measures of complexity. From this point on, they will be considered metaphors that will, hopefully, add clarity to the various facets of simplicity, which will be defined in the following section.

– *Shannon's entropy* measures a form of complexity related to unpredictability of systems described by probabilistic means.

– *K-complexity* formalizes the idea that complicated or random objects have long descriptions.

– *Bennett's logical depth* formalizes the idea that organized complexity is ultimately related to a computing effort needed to produce an object.

We can perhaps argue that the above concepts are not much more than common sense. We think, however, that the fact that part of our common sense can be formalized into some universal concepts is quite relevant and even rather unexpected. These three concepts are to be considered cornerstone concepts that capture part of the semantic of complexity in its purest form.

Let us take stock of the main things we have learned on complexity from information theory:

– First of all, even in the very formal realm of mathematics, there is *no single concept of complexity* (or simplicity) that is relevant for all purposes. This will be all the more true for more practical definitions.

– The three examples have one point in common. They all formalize the intuitive idea that complexity is related to a *quantity or value of the information* contained in an object, a system or its description, *relative to some previously set goal*.

– Universal concepts of complexity are likely to be uncomputable in practice. Practical concepts of complexity, on the other hand, are likely to be applicable to very narrow classes of systems only.

– The uncomputability of complexity can be traced back to the *impossibility of finding optimal descriptions of a system*. This difficulty is inherent to the complexity and should not be attributed to a lack of knowledge or skill. Even if some care is in order here, not to draw improper analogies between mathematical results and the IT world, we can perhaps recognize in this intrinsic difficulty of finding optimal description, a metaphor of the difficulty of finding optimal descriptions of real ISs.

– There are at least two essential aspects of the complexity of a system. The first aspect is related to the length of its description. This is defined as the *complication* of the system. Random systems are always complicated. The second is related to the degree of organization that the system contains. This is called *organizational complexity*.

– Defining complexity in a sensible way always *requires choosing an appropriate scale*, or equivalently an abstraction level, for the description.

– Defining the *abstraction level* for the model of a system involves two things. First, defining what *information is to be considered irrelevant* at that particular scale. Second, what *amount of computation or design the model encapsulates*.

The following section will take on simplicity which, surprisingly, is much more than the opposite of complexity.

2.2. What does the design tell us?

Simplicity has become quite fashionable lately. The new motto "Less is more!" is gaining momentum in many fields, probably triggered by the issue of global climate change that prompts us to rethink our economic models to produce less and to recycle more. In the computing world, the most prominent examples are certainly those of Google and Apple products, which are well known for their simplicity. The former popularized minimalist web pages through its search engine page, which has a single-input field and one button. Actually, this minimalist solution became even more minimal recently when Google launched its instant search feature. Users have been freed from the remaining effort required to click on a search button; results are displayed on the fly, while the request is being typed. One-button devices, on the other hand, are *Apple*'s specialty. The *Apple* mouse, the *iPhone*, and now the *iPad* are no doubt all milestones in a quest for simplicity in design. The last 10 years have witnessed a strong evolution toward simplicity; the era where stereos were expected to provide many displays, buttons, and tuning possibilities seems to be over.

Simplicity sells even better for services than for goods. When it comes to changing their ISP, their bank or phone companies, most people try to balance the often moderate increase in service quality, offered by a competitor, with the hassle of the paperwork generated by such a change. More and more companies have realized this and currently offer to take care of this paperwork for their customers. Even administrations seem to slowly get the point of simplicity. Indeed, large simplification endeavors have been launched in this direction in various countries, with moderate success so far, but there is still hope.

Getting back to our topic, we realize that an IS combines the two aspects just mentioned. First, most interactions with an IS are performed through user interfaces whose usability is directly related to the perception of greater or lesser simplicity experienced by users. Second, an IS plays the role of a service provider, which should supply information quickly, reliably, and is expected to be a substitute for traditional paperwork. Unlike an administration, though, an IS is expected to respond quickly to changing requirements.

While the various aspects of complexity of an IS are naturally associated with additional costs, simplicity is more naturally associated with creating value and opportunities, by focusing resources on what really matters. As we shall see though, they are deeply related and one often implies the other. The relationship between simplicity and value creation, on the other hand, will be the topic of Chapter 4.

Just as for complexity, which was addressed in the previous chapter, simplicity is something most of us would consider intuitive. We would no doubt recognize something as simple, whether we are considering a manufactured object, a business process, or a user interface. Defining simplicity, however, turns out to be a much more difficult task. There are a number of reasons for that. First, there is the polysemic nature of the word "simplicity". This is actually no different from "complexity", as we concluded in the last chapter. Second, simplicity is even more subjective than complexity, which can be measured and quantified, at least in special circumstances. Simplicity depends more on perception and is thus intrinsically harder to evaluate than complexity. Finally, it seems very hard to define simplicity facets that are truly independent. As we shall see, they often largely overlap and, at times, they are even conflicting.

These two things: polysemy and subjectivity, are what make simplicity both hard to define rigorously and, simultaneously, a useful and powerful guide in any design process, whether we are dealing with manufactured objects, business processes, systems, human organizations, or even concepts. In a thought-provoking little book [MAE 06], John Maeda, a world-renowned graphic designer and computer scientist from MIT, suggested 10 laws of simplicity. They certainly should not be put on the same footing as the mathematical definitions of the previous chapter because they do not have the same universality as the former ones. They are more like a summary of best practices distilled by an expert in design. Even though most of Maeda's insights on simplicity concern real-world objects rather than systems, we think that some of them can be adapted to our present concern, namely ISs.

Applying ideas of simplicity to computing and software development is not new. The principles of the *Lean Software Development*, which are adapted from the Japanese car industry, have been advocated by the Agile[5] community for already some time now. Some of these principles overlap with ours and, when this is the case, we shall mention it explicitly. We consider, though, that from a conceptual point of view, John Maeda's approach is more insightful.

The various aspects of simplicity we highlight in the following sections apply to different categories of IT stakeholders. The three most important categories are:

– customers,

– in-house end-users, such as employees and business experts, and

– the IT teams in charge of maintaining and improving the system.

Keep these three distinct categories in mind when we touch on the relation between simplicity, complexity, and value in Chapter 3.

2.2.1. *Simplicity by reduction*

One obvious way to increase simplicity in any system is to remove useless or duplicate features. Truly useless features are rather uncommon in ISs. One commonly sees, however, duplicate communication systems or duplicate identity repositories (we do not, however, consider backup systems as duplicates). Such situations usually occur when a new system or a new feature replaces an older one without the latter being removed. This can end up creating twice as much maintenance work to perform. A situation that was initially meant to be temporary progressively develops into a permanent one. Maintenance or coordination tasks are then

---

5 Agile software development refers to a group of software development methodologies based on iterative and incremental development, where requirements and solutions evolve in parallel.

often done manually; they are error-prone and increase complexity without any real benefits, except perhaps in that a few people will be able to retain their old habits.

More significant, however, are situations where a genuine reduction in the number or scope of features (not just suppressing duplicates) could be beneficial. Indeed, keeping only essential features favors more focused work and increases the chances that users will fully master the tools they are using. Many applications are still designed to allow for a great deal of customization. The downside of this, is this flexibility and customization is that it is often attained at the expense of a thorough mastery of those tools by people who use them daily. Too often, the need for customization and flexibility is overrated, while the need for fully mastering IT-tools remains undervalued. We shall come back to these essential mastery issues in section 2.2.4. In short:

> Knowing fewer things and knowing them better is a good idea!

This motto applies to both IT and business users. Simplicity by reduction means:

– For developers: knowing a few technologies thoroughly.

– For business users: being autonomous on the range of tools they use daily.

Flexibility and customization can certainly favor high creativity in some cases but, too often, they just create randomness. Customization and flexibility features should thus really be kept only in those circumstances where creativity is clearly identified as a major factor for creating value.

A beneficial side effect of reducing the scope and the number of features is that those removed features are often also the most complex ones to implement and to maintain. In a way, all of these can be seen as an instance of the famous *Pareto principle*, which states that, empirically, 80% of the effects (contribution to the complexity of the system) are accounted for by 20% of their causes (those unessential features).

Under the simplicity through reduction label we can perhaps also place factorization and pooling of resources. However, we prefer to keep those under the simplicity through organization label discussed below. This is just the first example of overlapping aspects of simplicity.

Broadly speaking, simplicity through reduction can be related to the *Lean Software Development's* "Eliminate waste" principle, with waste being defined as something that brings no value to users.

Finally, in reference to the mathematical metaphors of the previous chapter, we can argue that simplicity by reduction implies reducing some of the K-complexities of the system. The description of the IS just got shorter and thus becomes easier to understand. It is also likely that some entropy, due to the weak predictability of manual maintenance operations, will disappear when duplicated systems are suppressed.

Simplicity through reduction is in essence a principle of sobriety.

2.2.2. *Simplicity by hiding complexity*

While reducing complexity by suppressing features or services from a system is an objective transformation, there are other more subjective ways to increase simplicity. Hiding complexity is such a means to create a useful illusion. Simplicity thus has an objective aspect, namely the reduction of complexity as described in the previous section, but it also has a more subjective angle that is by no means less important or less useful.

> Simplicity is definitely more than the absence of complexity. Hiding complexity can often be a useful illusion for users.

Hiding complexity is often related to removing constraints for users. Take single sign-on (SSO), for example. What SSO really does is free users from the constraint of logging into several applications.

More generally, computers are really nothing but machines for hiding complexity of computational tasks.

Hiding complexity means putting it far away. What we have in mind here is the SaaS[6] model for enterprise computing, whose principle is to outsource altogether the infrastructure of commodity applications to datacenters of services maintained by large service providers. We will have more to say about the SaaS model in section 4.1.2.

By contrast with *Simplicity through reduction*, this new form of simplicity usually has a cost in complexity that should be carefully weighed. Both the descriptional complexity (K-complexity) and the organized complexity (Bennett's logical depth) are likely to increase overall when complexity is being hidden. The description of the system will be longer and hiding its complexity requires more design input. To put it simply, hiding complexity will promote the creation of value but will also require more design; these costs and benefits should be carefully weighed.

---

6 SaaS is the acronym for Software as a Service.

The pertinent question to ask is: When is it really worthwhile to invest in more design to produce more simplicity? One answer is that the encapsulation should benefit to sufficiently many and for a sufficiently long time to compensate for the additional design effort that hiding complexity requires. We shall give another element of response once we have defined what we mean by *Simplicity through learning*, which shares a deep connection with *Simplicity through hiding complexity*.

For the moment, to better understand what the latter means, let us pick some examples for the three categories of users of an IS.

2.2.2.1. *Customers*

Hiding complexity from customers is vital for a company that sells or advertises goods or services through an online platform. To encourage customers to return, everything should be configured for them to navigate a site comfortably. Special attention must be paid to ensuring that all relevant information are easily accessible. The slightest difficulty in finding information might result in customers massively leaving for the competition. This is of course the fascinating subject of graphical user interface usability, a topic that would deserve its own book and which corresponds to the expertise of graphical designers.

2.2.2.2. *Business analysts*

To make sound decisions, business analysts need, in principle, to run complex queries on one or more databases. Most of them, however, have had no training with the SQL (Structured Query Language) language. Reporting tools and business-rule management systems serve to hide most of the technical complexities involved in writing such queries. Often, they provide some sort of graphical mechanism as a way to build moderately sophisticated business queries.

2.2.2.3. *IT personnel*

Hiding complexity takes on different forms for people in charge of maintaining an IS. For developers, hiding complexity corresponds to the software design pattern known as encapsulation of data in object-oriented programming (OOP). Encapsulation in this context means that data belonging to a class (in the form of private attributes) shall never be manipulated directly. The only way to manipulate data should be through operations (methods) that guarantee the coherence of that data. The complexity of maintaining the coherence of data is being hidden by those operations. Operations can then be used blindly by other parts of the code, which will thus be exempted from handling data inconsistencies. The concept of interface in OOP is nothing but a very precise specification of how complexity should be hidden for specific purposes.

More generally, hiding complexity is related to the concept of service. The concept of service is a rather vague one because it occurs at so many different levels of IS architecture. As we just described, a service can just be a piece of code, typically a class, which provides some functionality to other parts of the code. More loosely speaking, however, a service can also be any form of encapsulation of an existing functionality, which should be made more broadly available. A common solution is publishing services in an enterprise directory where they can be looked up.

There is yet another, more advanced, form of encapsulation in software engineering, which is represented by frameworks. Because it is closely related to simplicity through learning, we postpone our discussion of this subject until that relevant section.

2.2.3. *Simplicity through organization*

Organizing is most easily described as performing any kind of action that helps combat disorder. Disorder is to be understood here as the unstructured state. Roughly speaking, organizing a system thus means putting structure into something that initially does not have much.

In an IT context, there are a number of well-known factors that contribute to increasing the disorder in an IS until it becomes literally unmanageable.

– Accumulation of quick-and-dirty pieces of code.

– Diversity of technologies that need to be linked together.

– Progressive obsolescence of technologies.

– Progressive memory loss regarding what has been created, due to employee turnover.

– Absence of an overall modeling of the IS.

– Finally, the chaotic forces of politics often play a significant and even dominant role.

A thorough discussion of sources of complexity in IT will be the topic of Chapter 4.

At a more fundamental level, however, the most remarkable feature of disorder is that it tends to increase spontaneously, even without any apparent cause. This affirmation seems like a joke but in fact has firm foundations in physics. It was formalized during the 19th Century in the famous second principle of thermodynamics[7]. Thermodynamics prescribes limitations on how energy flows can or cannot occur between systems but does not provide an explanation for *why* the entropy increases.

---

7 The second principle of thermodynamics asserts that there exists a state function known as entropy and that, for an isolated system, this quantity grows until the system reaches its state of thermal equilibrium.

However, to understand how to fight disorder, we really need to understand the mechanism that lies behind this spontaneous increase of disorder. Despite the fact that this is a deep subject of theoretical physics[8], its essence can be grasped intuitively. Think of a complex system as being composed of a number of subsystems or parts. Statistically, there are overwhelmingly more unstructured configurations than structured configurations. In the context of IT, such a system could be a piece of code, for instance, and "being structured" would simply mean that the code does what it is meant to do.

> Disorder increases because, starting from a structured configuration, any random evolution is much more likely to end up in one of the less-structured configurations.

Briefly referring to section 2.1, let us recall that the Shannon's entropy was a measure of the amount of randomness present in a system. Let us denote the number of configurations available to a system by N. Assume for simplicity's sake that each of these is equally likely to occur: then, as is shown in Appendix 1, the entropy reduces to $\log N$. Hence, the more configurations available to our system, the higher its disorder will be, thus confirming our intuition.

> Organizing a system requires decreasing the number of possible configurations available to that system.

---

8 It is related to the question of explaining how irreversibility occurs in macro-systems.

It can also mean a slightly different thing, namely decreasing the number of possible configurations in the description of the system rather than in the system itself. How can we achieve this? Well, mostly by grouping or reusing various parts, either in the physical world of systems or, conceptually, in the realm of models and ideas. This question of reuse will be investigated, from a practical IT point of view, in the subsection "implementing simplicity" in section 4.2.

Prioritizing tasks is a form of organization as well, but one that concerns transformation of processes rather than transforming systems. Essential things first!

Organizational processes are typically slow because they require insight and careful thinking. There is unfortunately no science of organization, but recall from the previous chapter that *Bennett's logical depth* was precisely the mathematical metaphor for those forms of complexity that can only grow slowly.

Organizing a system means trading some randomness and/or some descriptional complexity for a more structured form of complexity.

Experience shows that organizing a system is an iterative process. When finished, it should result in a system whose description has fewer components than the original system. The system becomes more predictable and easier to understand as a whole, making it easier to modify if necessary. The ability to understand the system as a whole is essential and relates to the next form of complexity, which is discussed in section 2.2.4.

Finally, note that decreasing the randomness of software is also one of the aims of *Lean Software Development*, according to the motto "Decide as late as possible". Delaying implementation decisions as much as possible will results in decisions being based on more facts than speculations.

2.2.4. *Simplicity through learning*

Knowledge and understanding make complex things look simpler. They are both achieved through learning, the process by which the human mind creates an efficient mental map that applies to a category of problems. This mind map is indeed conceptually similar to the concept of a "good" model that we discussed in section 2.1.4: if the mind map is to be useful at all, it should not be too deep. In other words, this mind map should result from a substantial learning effort to be readily useful in a practical situation.

Among all the facets of simplicity we have touched on so far, this is probably the most intricate facet because it relates to nearly every other facet. When applied in an IT context, this is really where the entanglement between the technical and human aspects of an IS come into play.

We shall actually distinguish two aspects to the learning facet of simplicity. We claim that learning can either obviate the need to hide complexity or can help transform complexity from one form into another.

2.2.4.1. *Learning obviates the need to hide complexity*

The point here is most easily made using examples taken from IT: learning frameworks and learning some simple syntax.

1) The first example is taken from software architecture and concerns frameworks. Put simply, frameworks are nothing but pieces of software architecture that solve well-identified and recurrent design problems that should not be tackled anew on each project. An object-relational framework, for instance, helps construct the object-relational

layer of a software architecture, which relates a database to clusters of business objects. Similarly, an injection-dependency framework implements an aggregation mechanism, which guarantees that software components will remain independent of each other, thus ensuring future flexibility. In essence, each framework is nothing but an advanced means to hide algorithmic complexity. The amount of complexity hidden in such frameworks is often quite large. It is not uncommon that it represents tens of thousands of lines of code[9]. The reason behind this complexity is that the range of problems a typical framework intends to solve is very broad.

It is very important to realize, though, that hiding all this algorithmic depth does not come for free. To be parameterized properly, frameworks require a lot of specialized knowledge and experience, which is by no way intuitive and easy to learn. Moreover, frameworks often introduce a set of abstractions, which take some time to become familiar. The point we are trying to make here is that there are numerous situations in IT where using frameworks really represents a form of overkill, all the more so when the problems at hand are reasonably simple.

> Using frameworks in simple situations adds unnecessary levels of abstraction and configuration when explicit coding could suffice.

The message is thus simple: even in 2012, learning how to make explicit, plain-old SQL queries and how to manage transactions "by hand" is still useful and valuable; in addition, learning how to convert data from tables into graphs of business objects will also be useful and valuable.

---

9 The core of Hibernate 3.0 contains nearly 70,000 lines of code and over 26,000 lines of unit tests.

We shall come back more thoroughly to these issues later when we discuss abstraction in section 2.3.2.

2) The second example we have in mind to illustrate how learning can avoid the need to hide a lot of complexity concerns *graphical tools*. When designed properly, these are intuitive and user-friendly; hence, it is accepted by users. Since they require no prior technical knowledge, such graphical tools are really just sophisticated "complexity hiders".

Take Gmail, Google's well-known mail service. It offers very powerful search features. The simpler part of this is available in the usual way: through a standard form that the user has to complete. For the most advanced features, however, the user is kindly asked to learn a little syntax. This small investment in learning some elementary syntax will be rewarded by the time saved when creating such complicated queries as: get all mail between dates 1 and 2 that had no attachments but were starred items.

More generally, experience shows that designing graphical tools is often very costly. They often hide unsuspected quantities of technical intricacies in the generation of the graphics and in the various surface checks they imply. But there is good news: in many situations, this complexity can be handled quite efficiently by human minds instead! There is nothing wrong with graphical tools, we all like them, but the decision to build them should be carefully weighed against the more rustic alternative of having humans learn a little technicality.

We summarize the above discussion in the motto of sobriety below. We believe it corresponds to an essential aspect of simplicity even if it is often overlooked because of an exaggerated, and somewhat naive, faith in the possibilities of technology:

> There are many instances where encapsulating a lot of complexity in systems can be traded with significant gain for a moderate amount of learning by humans.

Computers are good at hiding complexity. Humans are good at learning complexity. Systematically relying on complexity hiding is a weak and bad idea. Human brains are still extremely competitive in fighting complexity by learning.

2.2.4.2. *Learning allows complexity transformation*

Coming back to the example of frameworks mentioned earlier, it should be acknowledged that there are many situations for which their use is fully justified. Such is the case when they are used for solving many complex issues that would otherwise require an unrealistic amount of expertise to be coded explicitly. But, again, this encapsulation does not come for free. The deep algorithmic complexity is partly converted into complex settings in the framework's configuration files and into a set of abstractions that will require some effort to learn.

Using the mathematical metaphors of the previous chapter, we could say that some *Bennett logical depth* (specialized expert knowledge) has been traded for more *K-complexity* (long XML configuration files) and higher abstraction.

We summarize the above as:

> Learning can buy transformation of complexity. Algorithmic complexity can typically be traded for complexity in settings plus a set of abstractions.

One of the *Lean Software Development* principles, namely "Amplify learning", also touches the learning process. Continuous learning is considered an essential feature of the development process. Learning concerns technical aspects. But equally important is how individuals get to know each other and to work together efficiently and form a team. Learning is also required from end-users who should "learn" what their precise needs are by trying out the successive product releases that are the deliverables of the iterations. To make this learning process efficient, another *Lean Software Development* principle: "Deliver as fast as possible", emphasizes that time between two successive iterations should be short. This promotes early feedback from users and better communication within the team.

This final remark regarding speed brings us naturally to the next form of simplicity.

2.2.5. *Simplicity implies time saving*

Whenever an interaction with an object, a system, an individual, or an organization helps us save time, we feel a sense of simplicity. Time saved is that much more time we can use for something else. Ultimately, it means more freedom. As with complexity, there are both objective and subjective aspects to this form of simplicity. On the objective side, a search engine returning a list of answers quickly provides a sense of simplicity. This is obviously related to performance and efficiency of IS.

Sometimes, however, the same sense of simplicity can be achieved by merely displaying a progress bar that indicates the remaining time in a given process. This subjective shortening of time belongs to ergonomics and we will not have much more to say on this.

2.2.5.1. *Lack of time*

Before going further, lets us note that time is linked to simplicity in another way. That is, lack of time translates, sooner or later, into lack of organization at some level of the architecture. This lack of organization, in turn, translates into an increased unpredictability:

> Each organizational task requires a minimal amount of time. Decreasing time below this threshold translates into an increased unpredictability in a system's behavior.

The most extreme form of unpredictability is of course chaos. Incidentally, the link between speed and chaos has actually been theorized by some essayists [VIR 09], who prophesize that our civilization is facing a "global accident" in the near future. Restricting this analysis to an IT context, the global accident is to be interpreted, more modestly but more realistically, as the collapse of the IS. These things do indeed happen.

2.2.5.2. *How simplicity saves time*

Now, let us look how the various forms of simplicity we have considered so far can contribute to saving time.

Reducing the number of duplicated systems implies a lower maintenance effort. Manual synchronization procedures will disappear, too. The system is likely to act in a more predictable way, thus saving time spent debugging paranormal-looking phenomena. Suppressing non-essential features from an IS allows and sometimes even constrains users to focus on the basics. As a consequence, these basics will be quicker to master.

Hiding complexity obviously saves a lot of time to those who benefit. Let us recall our examples: graphical tools and frameworks. To put things simply, hiding complexity provides saving in learning time. Ergonomics in a way is nothing but the art of instilling a sense of immediate familiarity that will exempt users from explicit learning.

Organizing complexity reduces the number of subparts of a system, which thus becomes more intelligible to the human mind and more predictable. The learning effort required to have a reasonable overview of the system as a whole is thus strongly reduced. When the need for changes arises, these will be easier and faster to implement.

Learning, at first sight, might seem contradictory with saving time. In fact, learning is better considered a form of time investment which, in the end, will provide some time saving.

2.2.6. *Simplicity needs trust*

We can either trust in people or trust in systems. What is the relation here to simplicity? As far as trusting in people is concerned, things are more easily analyzed when we look at the consequences of a lack of trust. Can we trust that people will not empty our bank account? Can we trust that people will not use our private communications for their own purpose? Can we trust that people will declare their proper identity when logging in to a corporate site? Sadly, the answer to all these questions is: of course not! The technical consequences of this gave rise to the subject of IT security and cryptography, which is notoriously one of the most difficult (and very fascinating) in IT.

> Generalized lack of trust in human behavior implies a whole layer of complexity in the IS: "security".

Lack of trust implies designing many verification mechanisms:

– Checking a user's *access rights*, namely that he or she is granted the appropriate rights to access a resource.

– *Identifying* and authenticating a user implies checking that the user really is who he or she claims to be.

– *Non*-repudiation is ensuring that a user cannot claim to have not received a message that was actually received.

– Checking that a private message was neither intercepted nor modified goes under, respectively, *privacy* and *integrity*.

– Checking the signature of a message is asserting that it emanates from an identified source.

The above remark can be generalized in at least two directions. First, on the negative side, as the behavior of users cannot be reliably predicted, either because we doubt their competence or their moral integrity or both, additional checking mechanisms should be implemented. On the positive side this time, once we can trust someone, this simplifies his or her interaction both with systems and with other humans. The practical implications of this are not for the IS, which should be designed for average humans (those not trustworthy), but rather for the organization of teamwork and how to grant responsibilities. An organization can strongly benefit from trusted individuals.

Trusting systems reduces to reliability, a form of predictability that follows from simplicity through *reduction*, *hiding*, and *organizing*.

The *Lean Software Development principle* named "Empower the team" implies, among other things, that people should be trustworthy because this will favor reliable communication within the development team. This is sometimes summarized in the following aphorism:

> Find good people and let them do their own job!

As a visual summary, there are six simplicity principles that we will refer to later.

Figure 2.5. *Visual mnemonics or the simplicity principles: reduction, hiding, organizing, learning, time saving, and trust*

2.2.7. What does software architecture tell us?

Information theory has provided us with three deep metaphors of complexity. The laws of simplicity, on the other hand, as proposed by designer John Maeda, inspired six facets of simplicity. Introducing complexity through these non-IT perspectives had the advantage of providing us with a deeper understanding of the nature of complexity and simplicity. Rushing into IT specifics would never have allowed such a broad view. However, as was particularly apparent from our trip into information theory, there is a price to pay for this depth and generality, namely the non-computability of complexity. By contrast, jumping now to the much narrower topic of software architecture will provide us with examples of computable complexity.

Closely examining software architecture is motivated not only by the examples of computable complexity it provides, but, more importantly, by the need to mitigate the source of complexity that it represents within an IS.

> Software architecture is an essential contributor to IS complexity that it is important to understand and mitigate.

Section 2.3.1 examines two examples of computable complexity that apply to code and the IS architecture as a whole. Then, in section 2.3.2, we discuss the role of abstraction in code, how it is either part of the problem of generating needless complexity or, contrariwise, when it actually promotes simplicity.

2.2.7.1. *The complexity of code and of IS architecture*

The technical architecture of an IS can be considered a generalization of software architecture. Therefore, understanding what complexity means for the latter will help understand better what it means for the former. Our first example, *cyclomatic complexity*, will be specifically about the complexity of a piece of code of a function or software module. The second example, *scale-invariant complexity*, applies to general, multi-scale software architectures.

The literature on code complexity is actually quite impressive, if not for its quality, at least for its extensiveness[10] [DUG 05]. Any reasonably thorough review of the subject could easily require a book of its own. The two simple concepts we have picked out, cyclomatic complexity and scale-invariant complexity, have the advantage of being easy to compute practically. Moreover, they both illustrate the price to pay for concreteness, namely some arbitrariness

---

10 A summary of metrics for code complexity with an extensive bibliography can be found here: Mesure de complexité et maintenance de code by Philippe Dugerdil, Geneva School of Business Administration. http://lgl.isnetne.ch/isnet72/Phase3/complexiteCode.pdf.

in their definition. Investigating the scale-invariant metric, we also give ourselves the opportunity to propose a practical definition for the concept of scale we introduced earlier. What both examples have in common is that they perform a combinatorial analysis of the information flow within a set of components.

To streamline reading, the more technical details are deferred to Appendix 2.

2.2.7.1.1. Cyclomatic complexity

Among the myriad metrics of code complexity available, cyclomatic complexity is probably the best known. Most code analysis tools allow its measurement. In short:

> Cyclomatic complexity aims at measuring the amount of decision logic encapsulated in a software module or a function.

Cyclomatic complexity is best defined by associating a control-flow graph to the code under consideration. An example is given below:

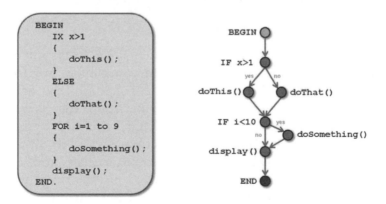

Figure 2.6. *The flow graph associated to a piece of code containing one decision and one loop*

This control-flow graph represents all possible execution paths through module. Cyclomatic complexity C_{cycl} is defined as follows:

C_{cycl} is the minimum number of independent paths through the control-flow graph that can generate all possible paths by mere combination.

This perhaps abstract-looking definition of C_{cycl} fortunately turns out to be very easy to compute. If E and N denote, respectively, the number of edges and nodes in the control-flow graph, then it can be shown that

$$C_{cycl} = E - N + 2.$$

Many books actually take the above as the actual definition, but this really obscures the true combinatorial significance of the cyclomatic complexity in terms of independent paths.

Practical wisdom has suggested that a module should not have a cyclomatic complexity much larger than 10. There is substantial evidence that beyond that limit the code becomes just too complicated to be maintained reliably.

2.2.7.1.2. Scale-invariant complexity

Recall that one of the main conclusions from our quick tour of information theory was that complexity, regardless of how it is defined, requires the specification of a scale of description of the system under consideration. ISs, obviously, have many scales of definition that, roughly speaking, correspond to the various architecture levels traditionally referred to in IT: business-process architectures, application architecture, software architecture, physical-deployment architecture, and so on. The question then naturally arises: "Faced with a multi-scale description of an IS, is it possible at all to define a measure of complexity for IS that would be

both computable in a reasonable time *and* scale-invariant?"
Even though it is by no means obvious to us
that scale invariance is truly desirable, the question, at
least, makes sense. The short answer to this question is: yes.
We now briefly present such a complexity measure as an
example of the arbitrariness involved in defining computable
complexities. It was proposed by Yves Caseau *et al.* [CAS 07].

To define a scale-invariant measure more formally, the
first step is to define a mathematically practical abstraction
of a multi-scale architecture. *Recursive graphs* do just this.
They can be thought of as a set of nested graphs at different
scales. Rather than giving a formal definition, we simply
describe it using the figure below. This is discussed in more
detail in Appendix 2.

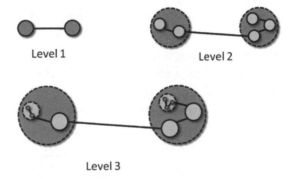

Figure 2.7. *An example of a recursive graph with three levels*

As a practical illustration of the above definitions we
propose the following:

– G_1 could represent a high-level SOA overview of an IS
considered as a set of services.

– G_2 could represent how services coordinate existing
applications to do their work.

– G_3 could represent the software modules that comprise
each application.

To discuss scale invariance, we also need a formal concept of the zoom-in and zoom-out operations on a recursive graph. When we zoom out, the low-level, small-scale details become blurred. When we zoom in, small-scale details reappear. This too can be formalized. Technical restrictions apply, however, to the admissible set of recursive graphs.

It is then assumed that each node of the recursive graph is characterized by a *unit cost of complexity*. These weights must meet a simple compatibility condition: the weight of a node at a given scale should be the *sum* of the weights of the (smaller-scale) nodes that it contains. It is by no means obvious that such a condition actually holds in real IT systems. However, this condition is essential for the definition below to make sense as a scale-invariant measure.

Let v_j denote the jth node in the smallest scale graph within the multi-scale graph. Let $(v_1 ... v_p)$ be a path of length p (i.e. an order sequence with possible repetitions of length p) on these nodes. Let $w_n(v_j)$ denote the weight of the node v_j. The explicit formula for the scale-invariant measure of complexity is then defined using a sum over such paths of length p:

$$\text{Scale-invariant complexity} = \sqrt[p]{\Sigma_{\text{paths}}\, w_n(v_1) ... w_n(v_p)}$$

The integer p is arbitrary, each value giving a different definition. The actual proof that this expression is really scale-invariant under the above zoom-in and zoom-out operations relies on elementary combinatorial analysis, detailed in the Appendix 1.

To make the above definition slightly less cryptic and to gain some insight, let us look at two extreme examples.

Figure 2.8. *The spaghetti graph and the hierarchical graph*

2.2.7.1.2.1. The spaghetti graph

As a simple metaphor of a maximally messy IT architecture we consider a graph where n nodes are connected with all other nodes. Set any p and take equal weights $w_i = 1$ on all nodes for simplicity. We must sum over paths *with* repeated vertices; each node v in the path $(v_1, \dots, v_p)$ can be chosen independently. There are n^p of them, from which we conclude that

Scale-invariant complexity of the spaghetti graph
$$= (n^p \cdot 1)^{1/p} = n$$

2.2.7.1.2.2. The hierarchical graph

As a simple metaphor of a more organized IT architecture consider $G_{\text{hierachical}}$ as mentioned above. Once a starting node v_1 has been chosen (there are n possibilities) each node v in the path $(v_1, \dots, v_p)$ can be chosen in at most four different ways, we now have

Scale-invariant complexity of the hierarchical graph
$$\leq (n \cdot 4^p \cdot 1)^{1/p} = 4n^{1/p}$$

Take $n = 100$ and $p = 2$ in the above formulas as an example. The complexity of the spaghetti graph is 100, while the complexity of the hierarchical graph is less than $4\sqrt{100} = 40$. This is actually true for any large number of nodes n and accounts for the intuitive fact that spaghetti architectures are messier than hierarchical architectures.

The lesson to be learned here is that there is a (high) price to pay for computability: artificial constraints have to be imposed on the structure of the admissible graphs and on the structure of the weight functions. This is to be contrasted with the deep and intrinsic definitions of complexity given in section 2.1.

2.2.8. Abstraction in software engineering

2.2.8.1. *Abstraction is everywhere in software*

Abstraction is at the core of software engineering. The reason for this is easy to understand: on a human scale, the tasks that software performs are best described in natural language. At the other end, however, processors have to deal with binary sequences. To fill this gap between the machine world and human scale, a range of abstractions, languages, and notations have been designed over the ages: assembly language, structured programming languages, OOP, APIs, patterns, modeling languages such as UML or BPMN, and so on. Computer specialists thus encounter many levels of abstraction daily, whether they are aware of it or not and whether they like it or not! As it happens, people hold strong and opposing views regarding abstraction. Some venerate it, while others abhor it. We shall come back to these more psychological aspects at the end of the following section.

2.2.8.2. *Depth and scale revisited*

In section 2.1.4, we concluded that the abstraction level of a model (of, e.g. an IS) is essentially defined by a *scale of description* of a system and a *level of compression* of information. Let us have a closer look at how both are interdependent. The scale of description is intuitively related to the amount and the nature of the information that is left out from a description or a model. However, information can be left out for very different reasons:

– The *information is irrelevant* to the current level of description.

For instance, when modeling business objects in an analysis UML class diagram, the programming language is of no relevance. Any information related to language specifics will (and should!) be left out.

– The *information is relevant* to the current level of description but is assumed to be otherwise *easily accessible*.

For instance, when modeling business objects in a design UML class diagram, the precise Java type of each attribute might not be explicitly specified because rules have been agreed upon on how to map generic UML types to Java types.

In information theory language: the *decompression to perform is moderate* because the model is shallow.

– The *information is relevant* to the current level of description *but is not yet explicitly known*. Some information is still to be found or created or designed.

Consider again an analysis UML class diagram, modeling business objects. At the time of modeling, the exact cardinalities at each end of the associations might not be known, even if they will be very relevant in the end.

In information theory language: the *decompression to perform is important* because the model is deep.

It is quite natural to try classifying the various abstraction levels, going from the less abstract to the more abstract. As it happens, this is less obvious than it looks. Consider, for instance, the three following abstraction levels:

1) UML diagrams used while *defining requirements* of an application (commonly known as the analysis phase). These diagrams usually formalize the functional requirements using a set of diagrams such as use-case diagrams and business-object diagrams and identify perhaps a few services.

2) UML diagrams used for *designing* the IS, on the other hand, are typically much more detailed and will also include details on the associations between business objects and signatures of methods in each service.

3) The *code* used in the programming language to build the application. By definition, code is explicit and leaves out no information.

If we decide a language is more abstract the more it leaves out a large amount of information we would conclude that:

> Abstraction(analysis diagrams) > Abstraction(design diagrams) > Abstraction(explicit code)   [2.1]

This is typically how abstraction levels are organized in UML textbooks. Suppose now we would like to classify the natural language, for example, when used to describe business requirements, according to the above criterion. Natural language embeds much implicit information when compared to explicit computer code. According to our previous rule we should then write:

Abstraction(natural language) > Abstraction(explicit code)
[2.2]

This, however, looks strange and counterintuitive. Indeed, common sense correlates abstraction of a language or of a notation with a sense of remoteness from our daily intuition. It seems our intuition thus combines scale *and* compression in a non-obvious way to produce a sense of remoteness. The human mind has different abilities to *decompress* various kinds of information. It is much more efficient to decompress information from natural language than from UML analysis diagrams, which explains the apparent contradiction between [2.1] and [2.2].

This is not a problem, however. It is rather a hint that:

More abstraction is not necessarily better or worse. The level of abstraction that is used should be appropriate for the problem at hand.

We will come back to this shortly.

2.2.8.2.1. Object-oriented programming

There is no doubt that OOP is currently the most common paradigm in programming. It introduces a set of abstractions and concepts that are well known to most programmers (classes, interface, heritage, polymorphism, etc.). Let us recall here that the initial goal of OOP was to provide a way to build large software applications by aggregation of smaller modules, while previous approaches, like structured programming, emphasized the opposite approach, namely decomposing large software into smaller modules.

The set of abstractions that OOP introduces is rather small and quickly mastered. It is grossly inadequate, however, to address most problems posed by enterprise computing. For this reason, the original OOP set of abstractions has been consistently extended following a now-standard scenario:

1) A set of *basic abstractions* on top of OOP, *known as APIs*, are defined to wrap the most common computing tasks such as building graphical user interfaces, connecting to databases or to directories, building persistence mechanisms, handling strings, reading and writing files, and so on.

2) The above APIs are often so complex that they require real expertise to be put to good use. This expert knowledge is then translated into a catalogue of *software patterns*. A pattern is most easily defined as a documented formalization of one best practice in software engineering, specialized to OOP[11]. The UML notation is used most often for this.

3) But software patterns are not yet software! There is still a long way to go from patterns to their actual implementation. This is where *frameworks* come into play: they supply reference implementations of some particularly important patterns. Currently, there are frameworks for patterns such as the MVC[12], IoC[13], or DAO[14]. As we discussed in section 2.2.4, they encapsulate expert knowledge that is being traded for some significant amount of parameterization and abstraction.

4) Now, even with frameworks available, writing robust code is still not an easy task. One approach that has been recently advocated is *model-driven architecture* (MDA) where explicit coding is replaced by designing UML diagrams. These will be converted into explicit code for specific platforms and specific frameworks.

This stack of technology, tools, and abstractions is by no means trivial to master. It requires quite a substantial effort, intellectual autonomy, and conceptualization abilities to be properly mastered.

---

11 The Core J2EE Patterns is such an example. http://java.sun.com/blueprints/corej2eepatterns/Patterns/.

12 MVC stands for Model View Controller pattern, which encourages the separation of user interface logic, business logic, and the data they operate on.

13 IoC stands for Inversion of Control pattern, which helps build software using modules that are strongly independent from one another.

14 DAO stands for Data Access Object pattern, which is a pattern for abstracting data manipulation within any data repository.

> Each additional layer was initially designed to simplify and rationalize repetitive tasks. At the same time, each layer brings its own complexity to software architecture. When is the balance really positive?

This is the central question that we tackle in the next section.

2.2.8.2.2. Good or bad abstraction?

When used properly, the introduction of a set of abstractions in software engineering can significantly contribute to mitigating many of the recurring problems in IS:

– *Improving code quality*. The encapsulation of expert knowledge in frameworks, using a set of well-conceived abstractions, promotes code quality, especially when used by beginners who otherwise would have to write, test, and debug such code from scratch. In principle, the uniformity of the code will be increased, thus maintainability will be improved as well, because many developers will have some knowledge of the most current frameworks.

– *Promoting the openness of the IS*. Opening the IS to other applications or other ISs can be achieved in basically two ways. First, web services can be made available that wrap part of the existing functionality of the IS to make it available to the external world. Web services are most easily described through WSDL[15] documents that are an abstract, technology-independent description of their functionality. Next, APIs are another way to open a system to provide tight integration of an external application into existing code. In a way, APIs can also be considered a network of contracts (interfaces) that precisely describe how to interact with existing code. In short:

---

15 WSDL = Web Service Description Language.

> Opening an IS is made possible by defining abstractions or contracts that describe how the outside world is allowed to interact with it.

– Protection against the fast pace of technological evolution. The idea of a contract, which is a particular form of abstraction, is also an essential way to allow a technology or an algorithm to evolve and improve, while keeping existing functionality stable. The set of interfaces make up the stable part of architecture, allowing the underlying implementation to progressively improve in reliability and performance.

The above arguments are the most often-quoted reasons for promoting the use of frameworks. Other approaches, such as MDA, promote "raising" abstraction by using platform-independent models and diagrams, the so-called PIMs. The idea then consists in building IT systems through modeling rather than the traditional way, through coding. Models and diagrams are indeed expected to be more natural to the human mind than computer code.

Confronting the above arguments with real-life projects shows that things are not really that obvious. It is by no means true, for instance, that more abstraction is systematically the way to go. Quite on the contrary, there are serious drawbacks to excessive or misused abstraction that cannot be overlooked. We now briefly discuss them.

– Multiplication of abstraction layers *can needlessly complicate and obscure the code* for simple tasks. Frameworks are usually created to solve intricate technical issues. One example is solving O/R mapping problems in a transactional and distributed setting. Another is structuring code in a modular way using the IoC pattern. Most often, frameworks also include security features and these bring their own complexity. There are many circumstances, however, where such tools are overly complicated and could profitably be replaced with more explicit and basic coding that bypasses the whole framework stack.

– Relying too much on frameworks and their set of abstractions can promote the dangerous illusion, for developers, that many of the basic programming skills, such as an operational knowledge of the basic patterns, have now become obsolete. The framework will take care of everything. In the worst case, the original rationale of a framework will be forgotten by developers. They will use it... just because it is there and it is the tradition to use it! In the end, the consequence of such blind and *indiscriminate use of frameworks' abstractions will be a progressive loss of basic technical skills*. This matter of fact exacerbated by the belief that computational resources are for all practical purposes limitless. Thus, the basic idea that the complexity of a solution should be reasonably proportional to that of the problem it addresses is progressively lost and, along with it, a healthy intuition regarding the performance of ISs. We will come back to this in section 4.3.2.

– As we have already discussed in section 2.2.4, frameworks really provide a special form of complexity hiding or, more accurately, a form of complexity conversion:

> Learning (a framework) can buy transformation of complexity. Typically, algorithmic complexity (or coding expertise) can be traded for complexity in settings, plus a set of abstractions.

As is implicit in this statement, the conversion does not come for free. Some learning effort is needed before the complexity encapsulated in a framework becomes relevant, in the sense that it provides effective time saving. This is just a restatement of the principle of *simplicity through learning*. It is thus essential that this learning period, which could span several weeks or months for some complex frameworks, be compared with other relevant timescales:

1) The first timescale is related to the *sustainability of the framework itself*. Modern, popular frameworks are now most often developed by the open-source community. They are quite stable, well-documented, and have a lifetime that largely exceeds the learning time. There is thus no real worry about their sustainability. By contrast, many frameworks have been and still are developed in-house. These often will not benefit from such sustainability, as they are often related to eccentric, temporary, and local technological endeavors. They are currently a major cause of needless complexity in ISs.

2) The second timescale to consider is related to the *period during which this framework will be used,* once it has been reasonably mastered, either by an individual developer or by an IT team. In other words, the rate of reuse is an important parameter to consider as well. For the learning investment to be reasonably profitable, the framework in question should be used more than once. As a rule of thumb, we can consider that using a technology or a set of abstractions only once is a waste of time and energy.

> There is a first time for everything, but there shouldn't be only first times!

As we can see, there is thus no quick and easy answer as to the usefulness of a set of abstractions. But three timescales should to be kept in mind and compared:

– The *time* needed *to fully grasp a set of abstractions.*

– The *sustainability of a set of abstractions,* which determines for how long they will be around.

– The effective *rate of reuse* once they have been learned.

These should all be lucidly balanced before making a decision to add any abstraction layer to the software architecture, if needless complexity is to be avoided. Such a sound decision is, however, often made quite difficult when most IT skills come from external software engineering companies. Developers hop from one project to another and face such a large number of technologies that they cannot afford to really master any of them in depth. Most often, they just adapt to an existing technical ecosystem of which they have no clear overview. They end up blindly complying with some local development rules or habits. Often, these were not really thought through, but rather emerged in a specific context. For various reasons (technology hype and local politics) those rules, in turn, often change too quickly to become part of a genuine technical culture which, alone, could turn them into efficient tools.

We shall come back to these important issues in section 4.3, when we discuss human factors to uncontrolled complexity.

2.2.8.2.3. Good abstraction is a form of simplicity!

API and frameworks respectively define and implement sets of abstractions (design patterns). "Good" abstraction is really a mix of various forms of simplicity principles as defined in section 2.2.

– "Good" abstraction *hides algorithmic complexity.* Frameworks are nothing but an advanced form of hiding expert knowledge on software design.

– "Good" abstraction *transforms complexity through learning.* Learning abstraction allows transformation of expert knowledge into a set of abstractions and some amount of parameterization.

– "Good" abstraction *saves time when designing software.* Provided the above balance between timescales is positive, a set of abstractions will indeed save time.

> Good abstraction, in the end, is nothing but a means of economy of thought. In no way is it a goal by itself.

Abstract thinking also plays an important role in IT, even *before* actual coding can begin, namely during the most delicate period of an IT project, analysis, which consists of transforming a set of user requirements into a design model that can, in turn, be unambiguously transformed into code. Referring to the definition we gave in "Depth and Scale Revisited" for an abstraction level, we can identify at least three levels of abstraction to be used in the delicate process of formalizing user requirements. We assume for simplicity's sake that the modeling is performed using the UML notation.

1) The level we call "Non-formalized what". This level corresponds simply to a set of requirements as they can be expressed by expert users, that is, in natural language and with no formalization whatsoever. These still contain ambiguities and implicit assumptions that should be clarified in later stages. A set of requirements is usually obtained as a summary of several interviews of expert users. This non-formalized level can hardly be avoided because it cannot reasonably be assumed that all users will master UML or an equivalent modeling language.

2) The level we call "Formalized what". This is where the formalization of requirements comes in. It is traditionally called the *analysis stage*. All ambiguities as to what exactly the system should be doing must be raised. The set of UML diagrams that are useful at this stage are typically *Use Case* and *Activity Diagrams* that help define a logical partition of the set of requirements, *Class Diagrams* that define an appropriate set of business objects and a set of business services that will make up the system. This level of description also typically includes a detailed description of the user interface as well as the navigation logic between

screens or windows. This level contains no technical information whatsoever.

3) The level we call "Formalized how". This is the level of description of a system that is appropriate for a software architect. It specifies how the system will be realized, which architecture choices are made, and which frameworks and APIs will be used. Detailed Class and Activity Diagrams are typically used at this *design stage*. This level contains all technical information left out from the analysis stage. This level may also include information regarding physical deployment: which software runs on which node within a cluster of machines.

4) *Explicit code*. This is the level we discussed previously. It is itself subdivided into a range of abstractions that belong to the various APIs and frameworks that will be used.

Much more could be said, but we will not go into such detail here because that would be the topic for a book on UML modeling. The main point that we would like to make is directly related to abstraction:

> The danger in the process of converting a set of requirements into a running application is not related to abstraction by itself but rather to the number of unclear abstraction levels that are being used in this process.

Let us explain this briefly, assuming UML is being used. The issue is that a notation such as UML, although it specifies as many as 13 different types of diagrams, does not specify clear and universally accepted abstraction levels. As a consequence, there is often much ambiguity left as to what, for instance, a class diagram really means. A business expert might expect it to provide a detailed glossary of business objects, whereas a developer will instead expect to find detailed information regarding the type of the attributes and the associations that should exist between classes being coded.

Experience shows that these kinds of ambiguities are a source of much incomprehension, especially among inexperienced IT teams. There are only two remedies for this:

– The first is to *define very clearly what kind and detail level of information a particular UML diagram should contain* at a given abstraction level. It is quite useful also to define how diagrams should be related to each other. How should *Use Case Diagrams* be related to *Activity Diagrams*? Should *Class Diagrams* at the analysis stage contain attributes? If so, should the attributes be typed? When should data be modeled as an attribute of a class or as an association of a class? There is no simple and easy answer to these questions. However, each IT team should define its own and stick to it.

– The second solution is to *keep the number of abstraction levels* (except explicit code) *limited to no more than three*. A typical mistake is that technical details and issues creep into the analysis diagrams where they have no place. In sum:

> The number of abstraction levels should be limited to the three above, excluding explicit code. Each should be clearly defined using examples and/or templates.

This way, communication between the business experts and the IT teams will be more reliable. Again, achieving such efficient communication between technical and non-technical personnel staff will not usually happen overnight. It typically requires the establishment of an enterprise-wide IT communication culture, with appropriate training of IT teams and business analysts led by individuals that have both good conceptual skills (to master UML and train their colleagues) *and*, simultaneously, a good knowledge of the business process (to illustrate concepts with relevant examples).

2.2.8.2.3.1. MDA and abstraction

Let us briefly come back to the MDA approach that we referred to earlier. Recall that the purpose of MDA is to build ISs using UML models (the PIM[16]) rather than by explicit coding. We can now rephrase this as an attempt to jump from the "Formalized what" level (no. 2) directly to the code level (no. 4) by automatic code generation. Thus, MDA implies, in principle, skipping the "Formalized how" (no. 3) level altogether. We remain extremely skeptical about the possibility of such an endeavor. First, because the MDA hype has often raised false hopes that applications could soon be generated by sketching a few diagrams and then pushing a button to generate code. We think these are not much more than naive daydreams, at least if MDA is to be considered as a general-purpose tool. The second reason for our skepticism is that there are no serious indications that building the so-called PSM[17] model (as a substitute to the level no. 3) is really simpler or more reliable than good old explicit coding.

2.2.8.2.3.2. DSL and abstraction

We conclude this long section on abstraction with a few slightly more speculative ideas that actually pertain more to ongoing R&D than to everyday project life. Most general-purpose software-engineering practices currently rely on the OOP paradigm. Objects are the single, basic abstraction on which all other abstractions are based: APIs, frameworks, and finally applications. This process implies successive encapsulation of aggregations of ever-more

---

16 PIM = Platform Independent Model.
17 PSM = Platform Specific Model is a set of metadata that defines how code generation occurs when targeting a specific platform such as Java Enterprise and .NET.

complex sets of objects. One possible explanation for part of the complexity of current IT is perhaps ultimately rooted in this implicit assumption that this basic object abstraction is *the* best possible foundation of enterprise computing. No doubt objects *can* be used in all layers of software architecture. They can be used to define such diverse concepts as a business object, a dynamic HTML tag, a transactional scope, a SQL request, a list of security credentials, or a GUI widget. Some of these uses of objects look quite natural to our intuition. Indeed, thinking of enterprise data as clusters of objects is rather natural. Other concepts, on the other hand, when expressed as objects, look rather contrived. Thinking about an SQL request, a list of security credentials or a transactional scope in terms of objects cannot be considered very natural, or very elegant. There is indeed a substantial learning effort (in the sense of section 2.2.4) that is associated with getting used to this "object-oriented way" of looking at things. Perhaps this effort could be avoided, or at least mitigated, provided the single object abstraction was replaced by a set of more specialized abstractions that would be targeted on different computing or modeling tasks. One language/notation could be used to express business objects, another could be used to express security credentials, still another to express nested transactions, and so on.

This is the so-called DSL[18] approach, which is currently still in its infancy. We consider that this approach is, by far, more promising and more lucid than the MDA approach. Many open questions certainly remain. For instance, we must ask how these different abstractions will be related to each other (this is really a generalized kind of O/R mapping problem) and how normalization will proceed, assuming such normalization is useful.

---

18 DSL = Domain-Specific Language.

Note that we used the word "elegance" earlier. Maybe this is actually a clue to be taken seriously. Other domains of fundamental or applied sciences, such as mathematics, modern physics, urban planning, or building architecture, have all made substantial progress by considering that elegance and beauty are to be considered seriously, especially when promoting simplicity and efficiency are at stake. Elegance is important in building architecture because we live in buildings. Elegance is important in mathematics because it is an unconstrained exploration of concepts. Computing, and especially enterprise computing, obsessed as it is by deadlines, has promoted short-term thinking and, so far, has overlooked this aspect of things altogether. Nothing indeed could sound weirder than a claim such as "What a beautiful IS!" Perhaps this is wrong.

Chapter 3

Value or Values?

You can't communicate complexity, only an awareness of it.
Alan Jay Perlis – Epigrams on Programming

The concept of value, for enterprise assets, is essential because it is a measure of their usefulness. Numerous concepts of values have been defined for enterprise assets. They can be categorized according to two main criteria. The first criterion is simply: "Who is concerned?" The second is whether the value is financial or non-financial.

The assets, in turn, are usually divided into *physical assets* and *intangible assets*. The former are the usual assets, those which can be seen and physically measured, such as buildings or machines. The latter, on the other hand, cannot be seen or measured directly but are nonetheless usually recognized as contributing to either the competitive advantage of a company or to its legal rights. In this category, we find assets such as trade secrets, copyrights, patents, human capital, and, of course, software. Some organizations[1] even propose ways to

---

1 International Accounting Standards Board (IASB).

account for intangible assets in financial statements and the literature on this subject is extensive.

Thus, we must ask what kind of asset an information system (IS) really is. An IS is actually a hybrid object. The hardware and the premises that house it are clearly physical assets. Remember also that an IS can be seen as the explicit knowledge of a company. Thus, an IS is also an intangible asset, just like human capital, specialized know-how, or patents. Some IT management methods are based on the idea that the IS is essentially an intangible asset whose financial value should be evaluated (see, for instance, [GIB 10]).

We must also ask which values are legitimate to describe the usefulness of an IS. It will come as no surprise that no single concept of value will do. We proceed in two steps. First, we review who are the main stakeholders of an IS and then propose a restricted set of values, both financial and non-financial. Second, we shall argue that the three non-financial values we retain, namely the *use value*, the *sustainability value*, and the *strategic value*[2] [BON 11] are independent from each other and describe an IS's usefulness for most stakeholders.

To put things into perspective, recall that our aim is to relate value to simplicity. Value is about defining appropriate quantities that measure the utility of an IS from the point of view of various stakeholders. In a way, it is a black-box view of an IS, whose aim is not to identify the sources of value. Complexity and simplicity, on the other hand, are identified as important parameters that underpin values. They are the explanation of *why* value is created or destroyed. It is a white-box view of the IS. The task of

---

2 Some authors use different terms for these two definitions. We refer to Pierre Bonnet's book [BON 11]. What is called "sustainability value" here is called "intrinsic value" there and what is called "strategic value" here is called "business value" there.

Chapter 4, once we have settled on an appropriate set of concepts of value, will be to connect this black-box view with the white-box view of simplicity.

3.1. Who is concerned?

Different kinds of people will be interested in different aspects of the usefulness of the IS. We distinguish below two categories of IS stakeholders: the internal stakeholders, those who belong to the company, and the external stakeholders, those who exist outside the company.

3.1.1. *Internal stakeholders*

There are four categories in this group. Each asks a different question regarding the IS.

– The Chief Executive Officer (CEO) asks: "Is the IS adapted to our enterprise strategy". The main interest of a CEO is to make sure that the IS is aligned with the enterprise strategy and that it will help differentiate the firm with respect to competitors, by promoting innovation for instance. The top management is also concerned with the contribution of the IS to the corporate balance sheet.

– The Chief Financial Officer (CFO) asks: "Are we making good use of our assets?" and "What is the contribution of IT to the balance sheet?" The primary interest of a CFO is cost control and an optimal allocation of resources: financial values are his main concern.

– The business management asks: "Do IT services meet our expectations?" This is mainly the point of view of end-users. Usability and productivity of business applications are their priorities. They also expect quick answers and fixes from the IT department in the case of problems or when requirements change.

– The Chief Information Officer (CIO) asks: "Is the IS sustainable and scalable?" The primary responsibility of a CIO is to provide IT services that will match user's needs now and in the future.

3.1.2. *External stakeholders*

In this category, we group users who are directly or indirectly concerned by the IS and who do not belong to the company. Some are only casual stakeholders (e.g. buyers, M&A (mergers and acquisitions) specialist) and some others only exist within regulated sectors (e.g. the Banking Commission for financial institutions). We distinguish four categories of users.

Investors include all stakeholders who are involved in asset management such as venture capital or private equity. These actors are primarily interested in evaluating the risks that IT puts on their investment.

Buyers are casual stakeholders whose main concern is to evaluate the impact of IT during a merger or an acquisition process. The criteria include the sustainability of the IS and the amount of work that will be required to integrate the IS of the acquired company with the existing IS.

Customers and providers are regular users who connect to the IS of the company. Their evaluation of the IS's usefulness is based mostly on quality of service, reliability, robustness, and the flexibility to meet new requirements.

Regulation authorities are public authorities in charge of enforcing regulations that are specific to some industries or that are related to the status of the company.

3.2. Concepts of value for an IS

As explained, no single concept of value will do. Therefore, the best strategy seems to define a small set of values, which, taken together, concern all stakeholders mentioned above. The first two concepts are important financial values, which are traditionally used in business accounting and when presenting a company's balance sheet. We give brief descriptions only for the sake of completeness, but will not use them later. The latter three are non-financial values and these will be our primary focus in Chapter 4 where we relate them to complexity. In section 3.3 we argue that these non-financial concepts are essentially independent, which guarantees that the information they globally convey is maximal.

The table below summarizes which stakeholder is concerned by which value.

	CEO	CFO	Business management	CIO	Investors	Buyers	Customers and providers	Regulation authorities
Book value		++		+				
Net worth	+	++		+	++			
Use value			++	+			++	+
Strategic value	++			+		+		
Sustainability value				++	+	++	+	+

3.2.1. Book value

This is a financial value and is therefore expressed in monetary units. In a sense, it is the simplest concept of value because it is based solely on evaluating explicit cost structures in the IS.

> Book value is defined as the total capital expenditure (CAPEX) plus the total operating expenditure (OPEX).

This is the concept used in projects when it comes to making trade-offs between different options. The book value is particularly attractive as it leaves no room for appreciation or subjectivity. It is also especially easy to calculate when compared with other more elaborate or more subjective concepts of value. However, it does not really represent the usefulness of investments as only directs costs and financial gains are valorized.

The book value has become popular primarily through the use of two indicators:

– The Total Cost of Ownership (TCO), which includes both the investment costs and the operating costs.

– The Return on Investment (ROI), which measures the time necessary for a project to amortize the initial investment.

The book value is certainly an important parameter to consider for CFOs but it cannot be used alone to arbitrate between various projects. The cost structure attached to an IS is indeed extremely complex and includes both tangible and intangible assets such as human capital, organization, knowledge, and software.

3.2.2. *Net worth*

This is the second most important financial value to consider. In general, and not only with respect to IT, there are three different meanings that are usually associated with this concept, depending on who is using it.

1) The *market value* corresponds to the price that can be obtained by selling a property. For an IS considered as a whole, this value does not make much sense, though, as there is no real IS market. It does make sense, however, for separate business applications.

2) The *liquidation value* is the price that can be obtained when some property has to be sold immediately. Obviously, this value will usually be much lower than the market value. For an IS, this liquidation value will correspond to material assets such as workstations, servers, and networking equipment. This meaning is the one which makes most sense for an IS.

3) The *replacement value* represents the total costs incurred for maintaining the business activity in a situation where the IS, or part of it, had to remain down for a longer period. Evaluation of this value is conceptually quite straightforward. Indeed, all that is needed is to evaluate the cost of replacement procedures. This line of thought has been followed at great lengths by various authors to propose a new and original way to manage ISs (see e.g. [GIB 10]).

We can summarize the above by stating that the net worth, whichever definition we choose, contributes to the statement of the financial position of a company.

Now, we come to three non-financial values that will be of more direct relevance to our purpose. These are the concepts that we shall connect with the ideas of complexity and simplicity that we developed earlier.

3.2.3. *Use value*

The term *use value* goes as far back as the writings of Karl Marx, Adam Smith, and even Aristotle's philosophy, on *Politics*. The concept thus has a very long history. In rough terms, use value measures the utility of consuming a "good". Adam Smith also opposes use value to the exchange value, arguing that a good, like a diamond for instance, can have exchange value but not use value. Water or air would be an example of opposite case (assuming there is a limitless supply thereof, which of course is questionable). Much has been written about the supposed objectivity or subjectivity of use value. Marx considered it an objectively determined value.

We will not review the whole history of this concept here. Our approach is to define a pragmatic concept of use value that is specific to an IS. The different stakeholders that we mentioned earlier may each have a different interpretation about what the utility of the IS should be. To establish an unambiguous definition of use value, we explicitly specify that the relevant stakeholders are the business users and the business management:

> Use value is a measure of the utility of the IS for business users and external business partners.

Most of the time, the use value of applications is considered, rather than the use value of the IS as a whole. The criteria we propose to take into account are described in the following sections.

3.2.3.1. *Functional criterion*

The *adequacy of the applications comprising the IS with respect to business processes* is the single most important functional criterion that affects use value. Imagine that a business process requires processing tasks in some specific order. Adequacy will imply that software should allow entering and processing data in order, which is natural to users. The adequacy, however, remains distinct from other, ergonomics, which we examine below.

3.2.3.2. *Non-functional criteria*

Ergonomics defines how well graphical user interfaces are adapted to the business processes. The general idea is that good ergonomics favors good working conditions. Ergonomics is about how elements are arranged on the screen and also about mechanisms for entering data (keyboard, trackpad, mobile devices, etc.). Poor ergonomics could also imply repeatedly entering similar data or entering useless data.

Performance is primarily about the response time of applications and about scalability when the number of users and volume of data increase. Poor performance has negative impact on working conditions and thus indirectly penalizes business.

Availability is the ratio of uptime for an application or a system. Clearly, downtime will have direct financial impact when critical business applications are involved.

Reliability is the ability of an application or a system to work properly without losing or corrupting data. Such problems could have severe consequences (losing money, negative publicity, and failure to comply with regulations).

Many of these criteria that contribute to use value have a more or less direct relationship with one or more of the simplicity concepts we described in Chapter 2:

– Simplicity by *hiding* plays an essential role in ergonomics, whose purpose is precisely to make interaction with complicated data feel simple.

– Simplicity through *time saving* plays an obvious role in ergonomics (the user interface should be responsive), in performance and in availability (the average recovery time should be short).

– Simplicity through *trust*, obviously, has something to do with robustness and reliability of systems that can be trusted to work without interruption.

Some authors have proposed to quantify use value financially, by evaluating the cost of manually performing part or all of the data processing that is performed by the IS. Although this approach is quite interesting, there remains a large part of arbitrariness in this option because it implies a significant quantity of subjective assessments that are gathered mainly from interviews of the different domain experts.

3.2.4. *Strategic value*

The *strategic value* measures the contribution of the IS to the competitiveness of the company. IT is a non-financial value. In other words:

> Strategic value measures how much the IS contributes to making the company different from others in the same market.

The strategic value is rather hard to measure in an unambiguous way. One possibility consists of classifying applications in an IS into three distinct categories:

Commodity applications such as mail, calendars, collaboration, and office tools. These are ubiquitous applications that are common to most companies today. They do not substantially contribute to making any difference with respect to competitors in the core business, as they are available for a moderate cost to all companies. Increasingly, they are simply SaaS applications offered by the major "cloud" players (Google, Amazon, Salesforce, etc.).

Commercial software packages or business applications are specific to some activity or business domain. They are not specific to a company, however, as is software that is developed in-house. One common mistake is to try and create significant competitive advantage by mere parameterization of commercial packages.

Business applications developed in-house are specific to a company. They are likely to provide most of the competitive advantages conferred by the IS.

There is no easy or obvious way to measure the strategic value. One possibility is to estimate the ratio of business applications, which are truly differentiating with respect to other companies. Another is to estimate the ratio of IT projects that correspond to significant business innovations.

The strategic value is not easily related to our primitive concepts of simplicity, at least directly. However, we will take that question on in Chapter 4 and show how the strategic value can be enhanced when fighting IT complexity.

The stakeholders who are most naturally interested in the strategic value are the CEO and the CIO as a partner of business users.

3.2.5. *Sustainability value*

Maintaining high levels for the use value and the strategic value should be considered the primary aim of any IT department. It is important to realize, however, that an IS with a good use value or good strategic value in the present does not imply that these levels will be maintained in the future. A poorly maintained IS could provide satisfaction to its users at a given time but performance could degrade quickly due to poor scalability or low maintainability.

Like a living creature, an IS is in permanent evolution. A balance is necessary between its robustness and flexibility. The ability to maintain high levels of use value and strategic value through flexibility is what we call the sustainability value. It is a non-financial value. The sustainability value, or sustainability in short, is a hybrid that takes into account many aspects of IT quality:

How well is flexibility designed into the IS? Flexibility is supported by a high level of modularity at all levels of the IT architecture: the infrastructure, the quantity of reusable services, and the quantity of reusable software components. A high level of modularity enables us to evolve an IS by composing existing modules. It is loosely related with *simplicity through organization*, which among other things implies minimizing redundancies.

Scalability is the ability of an IS to accommodate an increasing number of users by merely adding hardware resources. It is a specific form of flexibility with respect to increasing work load. It is directly related to *simplicity through hiding*, as scalability implies, by definition, hiding altogether the complexities related to pooling hardware resources.

The quality of the IT governance is important to guarantee that there exists a complete chain of responsibility that covers all aspects of IS evolution: the physical infrastructure, the logical architecture, and the software architecture. Loosely speaking, there is probably some relation with simplicity through organization again here.

Quality of *modeling* and *modeling processes* is essential for maintaining a consistent overview of what the IS contains. Having a clear map of the logical architectures, the flows of data, the services available, and the software architecture of each component is a prerequisite to any change of the IS, because it allows us to maintain increasing complexity under control. Consistent and systematic modeling guarantees that the memory of the IS architecture will never be lost, independently of who is in charge of the IT in the future. When no modeling is available and those who built the system are no longer available either, some archeology or reverse engineering work will be necessary before changes or extensions can be implemented. Modeling allows the creation of a mental picture of the IS, or part of it. It is thus directly related to *simplicity through learning* and the *time saving* it implies.

With regard to flexibility, our first point, one approach to its evaluation consists of comparing the current situation of an IS with a well-defined set of good practices, such as CMMI, ITIL, COBIT, or TOGAF. There are even tools, such as the IS-Rating tool, whose purpose is to evaluate the technical quality of the three basic middleware components of an IS:

– The MDM[3], for the coherence and maintainability of reference data.

– The BRMS[4], for the flexibility and traceability of changes to business rules. Business rules are understood here as a set of rules that are enforced to ensure consistent data integrity over time.

– The BPM[5], for the flexibility and traceability of changes of business processes

The assumption of the IS-Rating tool is that sustainability largely relies on the quality of these three middleware components.

---

3 MDM = Master Data Management.
4 BRMS = Business Rule Management System.
5 BPM = Business Process Management.

Summarizing:

> The aim of sustainability is to provide an evaluation of the robustness and the flexibility of an IS and its organization to guarantee its usefulness in the future.

The primary stakeholders who are directly concerned with the sustainability value are the CIO and any potential buyer: the CIO because he is in charge of insuring the robustness and the adaptability of the IS and buyers because they need to evaluate the integration costs of the IS into their IS.

In contrast with use value and strategic value, sustainability value is not an aim in and of itself but a means to ensure the sustainability of IT investments. It is a predictor for the evolution of the other two values in the near future.

3.3. Are these values sufficient and independent?

Use value mainly concerns business users and partners, while *strategic value* primarily concerns CEOs and CIOs. They are thus both needed, as they concern separate kinds of stakeholders. As soon as we acknowledge the need to evaluate the ability of the IS to cope with future changing requirements, and not just with present needs, we must add something like *sustainability value*. Not much doubt is permitted that this trio of values is indeed needed to evaluate the utility of the IS now and in the near future.

Figure 3.1. *Use value, sustainability value, and strategic value will be related to simplicity actions in Chapter 4*

The question which remains is: "Are these three concepts truly independent of each other?" We claim they are. The following table lists all possible combinations of these values, which are given nicknames:

#	Use value	Strategic value	Sustainability	Comments
1	KO	KO	KO	"IT chaos"
2	KO	KO	OK	"Tech academy"
3	KO	OK	KO	"Alignment trap"
4	KO	OK	OK	"Users are unimportant"
5	OK	KO	KO	"Business-user tyranny"
6	OK	KO	OK	"Wrong direction"
7	OK	OK	KO	"Architecture is a waste of money"
8	OK	OK	OK	"IS heaven"

These are only meant to identify extreme scenarios and thus illustrate that situations indeed exist where the three values are independent.

3.3.1. *IT chaos*

This is a state of unpredictability and non-sense. The best solution is likely to start building a new system from scratch rather than trying to fix or modify the existing system. Decisions will be made based mostly on financial considerations.

3.3.2. *Tech academy*

This scenario has become rather uncommon lately but it still exists in some places. In this situation, the architectural foundations are sound because the IT department is run by competent technical experts. However, focus is on technology alone, while forgetting that an IS is first and foremost a tool, not a technical playground, and that its primary purpose is to serve users, customers, and the business. Such a situation usually results from bad governance that has put too much power in the hands of tech teams.

The remedy is to completely reorganize the IS governance to give more power to the business.

3.3.3. *Alignment trap*

This situation occurs when a company has overemphasized the importance of the strategic value. Management thinks the primary goal of an IS is to be aligned with the enterprise strategy, with no consideration for the robustness and user satisfaction. This short-term vision prevents the definition of any robust architecture. All manpower is used to cope with the need for flexibility and handling ever-changing requirements. In recent years, many IT departments opted for service-oriented architecture (SOA) because they were obsessed by flexibility and alignment of IT with business processes. Huge amounts of money were invested into IT that never had time to become mature.

The *alignment trap* scenario was described in detail in a famous article from the Sloan Management Review from MIT [SHP 07].

The remedy is for the CIO to become aware of the specifics of IT. A global overhaul of IT governance is needed as well as substantial investment to consolidate the basic IS infrastructure.

3.3.4. *Users are unimportant*

This scenario is rather uncommon. It corresponds to a situation in which the IS is based on solid foundations and is also aligned with the company's strategy but the ergonomics of application is neglected and obsolete.

The remedy is to reorganize IT governance to include user representatives in the decision process.

3.3.5. *Business-user tyranny*

This situation is one where business users lay down the law. Current use value is high but there is no long-term thought for creating a robust and modular architecture that can accommodate future requirements. There is no strategy in the long run for developing specific applications with strategic added value. IT management is purely reactive.

The remedy is for the CIO to become aware of the specifics of IT. A global overhaul of IT governance is needed as well as substantial investment to consolidate the basic IS infrastructure.

3.3.6. *Wrong direction*

This is a rather common scenario in which the IS brings satisfaction to its users and has solid foundations. However, there is no real strategy to turn the IS into a key competitive advantage.

The remedy is for the CEO or another guardian of the organization's strategy to become more involved in IT governance.

3.3.7. *Architecture is a waste of money*

This is probably one of the most common scenarios. Although the IS is currently bringing satisfaction to business users and is bringing some competitive advantage with regard to other players in the same market, there is no guarantee that this situation will be maintained in the future. The IS has no robust foundations and no built-in flexibility. Future changes are likely to be either expensive or impossible without creating a new system from scratch.

The remedy is for the CIO to become aware of the specifics of IT. A global overhaul of IT governance is needed as well as substantial investment to consolidate the basic IS infrastructure.

3.3.8. *IS heaven*

This is definitely an uncommon situation. However, even those "happy few" will have to work to stay in this ideal situation.

Chapter 4 addresses the relationships between simplicity, complexity concepts, and our three independent measures of value: use value, strategic value, and sustainability value.

Chapter 4

Promoting Value Through Simplicity

Everything should be made as simple as possible,
but not simpler.
Albert Einstein

The stage is now set for connecting the concepts of
value, described in Chapter 3, with the ideas of simplicity
introduced in section 1.2. As a matter of fact, there is no
single obvious way to make this connection and we shall
therefore have to justify our approach. One thing to be
aware of is that the concepts of value and those of simplicity
introduced so far are not truly defined on the same
conceptual level. On the one hand, we have ideas of values,
which were defined specifically in the context of IT: *Use
Value*, *Sustainable Value*, and *Strategic Value*. On the other
hand, we have concepts of simplicity, which were defined at
a much more general level: *Reduction*, *Hiding*, *Organization*,
Learning, *Time Saving*, and *Trust*.

Part of the difficulty in linking value and simplicity lies in this discrepancy: we have concepts of value specific to IT while we have general and fundamental concepts of simplicity and complexity.

The most straightforward path would be to identify each concept of value from Chapter 3 as a function of one or more simplicity or complexity parameters. Actually, this is what we did, implicitly, in Chapter 3 when we related the *Use Value* and the *Sustainability Value* with some fundamental concepts of simplicity. Although this approach looks quite appealing, it appears too naive and does not immediately lend itself to a pragmatic framework for enhancing value, especially because of the above discrepancy.

Another strategy could be to attempt to define simplicity or complexity concepts that are truly specific to IT and then link those to the various values. Even assuming these ad hoc concepts exist, their relation with our earlier concepts could be quite obscure and thus of little practical use. Again, this approach would hardly lead to an effective framework for value enhancement.

For these reasons, we choose a more pragmatic approach in this chapter. First, we identify and logically organize the main sources of uncontrolled increase of complexity in IT. This probably introduces some arbitrariness in the approach, as other classification schemes could be considered equally legitimate. This seems, however, an inevitable price to pay to move from *simplicity principles* to *simplicity actions*. To keep things manageable, we chose to identify three main sources of uncontrolled increase in IT complexity, hoping that these will connect with the reader's own experience once we have defined them precisely. Explicitly, these main sources are *growing technical heterogeneity*, *changing requirements*, and a restricted set of *human factors*. We next identify primary causes that in turn are at the origin of the each main source. Having primary causes and main sources is merely a matter of organizing, as logically as possible, a range of causes that often overlap or even have circular implications. Finally, the concepts of simplicity will enter the analysis in two ways:

1) Simplicity principles will be associated with actions to *mitigate* the primary *causes of complexity* and hence also the main sources.

2) Simplicity actions will be identified as *opportunities to generate* different forms of *value* for the information system (IS).

This is pictured in Figure 4.1.

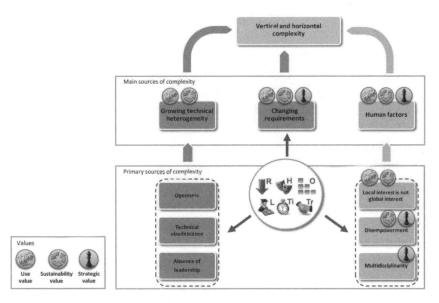

Figure 4.1. *Generation of uncontrolled complexity has three main sources: growing technological heterogeneity, changing requirements, and a number of human factors. Primary causes will be identified, which contribute to those main sources. Simplicity principles will be applied directly to those primary sources to mitigate their effects. We shall argue how these simplicity actions translate into creation of value, in relation to the sources of complexity on which they act*

These reflections also underlie the practical simplicity framework described in Chapter 5, where we examine how simplicity actions translate practically when we focus on specific architecture layers of an IS.

4.1. Growing technical heterogeneity

Among the many causes of uncontrolled IT complexity, growing technical heterogeneity is probably the most obvious cause. Put simply, technical heterogeneity refers to the fact that different technologies or tools are used jointly for similar purposes. This heterogeneity may concern the operating systems, business applications, or programming languages used for specific developments.

Here are a few common examples:

– Running *different operating systems* such as *Windows, Linux*, and *Mac OS* is a very common source of IT heterogeneity. With different file systems, different security models, and different ways to install new software, this is perhaps the most common source of IT heterogeneity. The *Java* language with its famous motto: "write once, run everywhere" was indeed originally created to alleviate this problem regarding specific developments.

– Using *different programming languages* such as *Java, .NET,* or *Cobol* for specific developments is another instance of technological heterogeneity. Even though each language is in principle universal, their coexistence within a given IS will usually imply numerous gateways, marshalling and un-marshalling operations as well as code wrapping. But from a business-operation point of view, this code is really do-nothing code.

– Having *different collaborative office tools* within one company, say *Microsoft Exchange, Google Apps,* and *Lotus Notes,* is another instance of technological heterogeneity. Each previously mentioned solution provides more or less equivalent mail and calendar services. But each solution comes with its specificities, which make the different tools not fully interoperable, hence the complexity.

– Even within a given layer of software architecture, there can be a great deal of heterogeneity. This is because *many APIs and framework are available for each technical task*. It is thus not uncommon to find several O/R[1] frameworks or MVC mechanisms used within an IS or even within a single application.

– *Middleware* and *infrastructure software* such as application servers, ESBs,[2] relational databases, or enterprise directories from different vendors also largely contributes to technical heterogeneity.

– Perhaps one of the trickiest forms of uncontrolled complexity is that which results from the *coexistence of several versions of the same product*, language, OS, or applications, as differences in behavior are usually very subtle and hard to track and fix.

For more clarity, we distinguish two kinds of macroscopic complexities (not to be confused with the information theory complexities) related to the plethora of technologies that coexist in an IS:

Horizontal complexity: we use this expression to refer to situations in which several *equivalent technologies coexist to perform the same tasks*. Tasks could be either technical or business-related. A typical example is one in which several brands of application server are running different applications.

---

1 O/R stands for Object Relational mapping. This is the software layer, which is in charge of converting the relational data model used in databases to clusters of objects used in object-oriented languages.

2 ESB stands for Enterprise Service Bus. It is a piece of software, which enables the implementation of a service-oriented architecture. It supplies low-level services such as routing logic, security, and monitoring.

Vertical complexity: we use this expression to refer to situations where *technologies are nested like Russian Matryoshka dolls*. Such a situation usually occurs as the consequence of an iterative use of the "simplicity through hiding" principle: a new layer of architecture wraps the previous one in an attempt to hide its complexity.

> *As an example, consider handling data in a relational database from within Java code. The first layer of architecture is the so-called driver that converts Java queries into queries specific to the database at hand. The Java API (JDBC) that defines how Java code interacts with an RDBMS can be considered the second layer. An O/R mapping framework on top of JDBC is yet another layer. As working with an O/R framework often involves performing much configuration and writing large amounts of boiler plate code, many development environments currently offer wizards that automatically generate most of this code and parameterization.*

Still other mechanisms take charge of the automatic creation of unit tests or the continuous-integration tasks during development and deployment. All of these nested layers of technology contribute to what we term "vertical complexity".

Technical heterogeneity has several worrisome consequences:

– *It increases the range of technical skills needed* to maintain an IS in operational condition.

– *It increases the amount of purely technical code* to perform conversions and wrapping tasks that have no business value.

– *It increases IT workloads by duplicating maintenance tasks.*

– It complicates the interdependence between subsystems, making the overall system less predictable and more difficult to maintain.

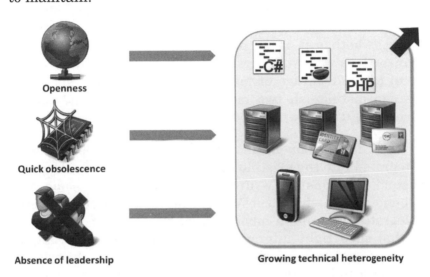

Figure 4.2. *There are three primary causes of complexity due to technical heterogeneity: openness, quick obsolescence of technology, and absence of technological leadership*

Impact on value

Generally speaking, significant *heterogeneity* strongly *decreases sustainability* value, as maintenance costs increase with heterogeneity. In extreme but not uncommon cases, a very high level of heterogeneity may even make maintenance impossible, as too many IT skills are required.

Heterogeneity usually brings with it unpredictability and unreliability, which may *negatively impact use value* regarding performance and availability of the system.

Let us now move to the primary causes, which explain why heterogeneity grows.

4.1.1. *Openness*

ISs do not exist in a vacuum; they are fundamentally open systems that must adapt to changing conditions. Most of them need to connect one way or another to the external world, whether it is to reach customers, to perform B2B transactions with suppliers, to exchange data with partners, or to take advantage of remote services. Roughly speaking, we can distinguish two modes of integration. One can be termed *tight integration* and the other *loose integration*.

Tight integration means that a service or application is integrated into the existing IS by adapting the code. Usually, custom code must be written that complies with some API, depending in which subsystem the new service is being integrated. The main advantage of this type of integration is that such tight interaction allows dealing with complex transactional and security contexts. This would otherwise be very hard to achieve by merely wrapping the new system in a set of stateless services.

The Java Connector Architecture *(JCA) provides an example of such a tight-integration mechanism. It defines various contracts for sharing security and transactional settings as well as handling connection pools.*

Loose integration, on the other hand, means that new services to be integrated are first wrapped and exposed as stateless services using only ubiquitous protocols and standards such as HTTP and XML.

As an example, the so-called REST *architecture style provides a way to define services in which the* HTTP *protocol supplies the basic operations (*GET, PUT, POST *and* DELETE*) for manipulating remote data.*

The primary advantage of this type of integration is its straightforwardness. When many services are involved, it will become necessary to define a pivot format of business objects, usually in XML, in order to maintain coherence, interoperability, and flexibility among the different services.

4.1.1.1. *Why complexity increases*

Let us summarize the various ways in which uncontrolled complexity can creep in, due to increased openness of the IS, and favor technological heterogeneity.

– If we are not careful, *the IS might become dependent on the inner workings of the new services* to which it is now coupled. Any functional or technical change in the newly included services could impact the existing infrastructure and require appropriate changes.

– Connecting to new systems can also imply *performing additional or enhanced security checks* to protect from malware or from possibly inconsistent data manipulation.

– Most often *encoding and decoding operations* are required, because the new system does not use the same vocabulary or business objects as the existing ones.

4.1.1.2. *Implementing simplicity*

Correspondingly, here is a list of general simplicity countermeasures that can be applied to mitigate the increase of complexity due to opening up the IS.

– To avoid creating dependencies on new systems, the classic solution is to *define a set of appropriate interfaces*. These interfaces are contracts that both sides, the existing IS and the new system, must comply with when exchanging data. This way, even if the implementation of the service changes over time, the contracts are stable and will protect from changes creeping into the existing infrastructure.

Of course, substantial functional modifications will still require changing these interfaces. Defining interfaces is really an instance of achieving *simplicity through hiding complexity*. It is also an instance of good abstraction as we have already discussed in section 2.3.2.

– When many services are added and required to exchange data, it is often very useful to *define an XML pivot format*, which specifies an official vocabulary that all services must share. Defining a pivot format will simplify subsequent integration of new services. The price tag can be quite high, however. Major harmonizing tasks unfortunately do not happen overnight and require many experts, often with different technical backgrounds, to collaborate over long periods. The endeavor is so significant that, whenever businesses-object models or XSD schemas or generic business processes have already been defined for an industry, they should be used or extended rather than developed from scratch. Defining a pivot format implies different forms of simplicity: *reducing* duplicated or overlapping concepts, *organizing* the remaining ones, and finally *learning* these concepts to implement them efficiently in new services.

– *Avoid exotic solutions as much as possible* in favor of straightforward ones based on industry standards such as XML. The REST architecture style is a good example of a robust and simple architecture. These solutions will be by far easier to maintain, because skilled employees will be easier to find and because they reduce horizontal complexity.

This is really *simplicity through reduction*.

4.1.2. *Rapid obsolescence of IT*

The pace of technological progress in hardware performance has been steady for about half a century now and it currently shows no sign of slowing down. It seems that Moore's law[3] will still be around in the years to come. Automatically, this fast pace of evolution favors quick obsolescence of IT, which in turn favors heterogeneity as versions of technology accumulate in layers over the years.

Let us review the three main mechanisms at work in this continuous obsolescence.

Obsolescence driven by performance

> New technologies replace older ones, pushed by the availability of more resources, by their compliance to newer standards and by algorithmic enhancements.

Newer versions of a technology typically offer more features, better performance, and include more of the emerging standards than their predecessors, sometimes even for a less significant effort and a smaller investment.

The successive versions of the Java Enterprise *platform illustrate quite well this path to obsolescence: the number of APIs has progressively increased to encompass nearly all aspects of enterprise computing and all industry standards and protocols. Some Java APIs are officially marked as "deprecated".*

This essentially contributes to *horizontal complexity* of IT as successive technologies usually perform equivalent tasks.

---

3 The most common version of this "law" states that computing power doubles every 18 months.

Obsolescence by driven automation

Repetitive tasks with low added value are progressively automated.

As more computing resources become available, more and more tasks can be automated. Repetitive tasks with low human-added value are automated first. Here are a couple of examples:

There are generators or wizards, *which generate much of the so-called boiler plate code in a software solution. This can include GUI generation and event handling, O/R tools or unit tests.*

There are also scripting mechanisms, *which automate tasks related to packaging applications in executable archives. Within the* Java *platform,* ANT *has been one of the favorite tools among developers especially because scripts now use the XML standard.*

There are tools which take care of many of the tasks related to project supervision *and continuous integration. Dependencies between various code archives are handled automatically, project supervision websites are generated to share information with all members of a team, depending on their responsibility, etc. Within the Java platform,* Maven *remains the archetype of this kind of project tool.*

Low-level tasks (writing HTML code, writing SQL queries, building a GUI, or creating project archives) are increasingly delegated to a set of automations. This progressive automation is indeed nothing but a form of *simplicity through hiding*. Arguably, we are thus witnessing obsolescence by hiding in the sense that the primitive mechanisms still exist but they are not used explicitly anymore. They disappear at the bottom of the technology stack.

The automation of low-level tasks thus essentially contributes to *vertical complexity* of IT.

Obsolescence driven by abstraction

> Low-level complexity is progressively wrapped within new abstractions.

Partly related to the above progressive automation process, there is a progressive wrapping of complexity in new abstractions.

Consider, for instance, the basic task, which is to create a dynamic web page using the Java *platform. At the bottom of the API stack, there is the possibility to write an HTML page explicitly as a plain string of characters and send it to an HTTP stream. As this quickly becomes tedious, the* Java *platform provides an abstraction of a request-response paradigm that underlies any web server. It is called the servlet API. But using this API still entails manipulating low-level HTTP concepts, such as writing to output streams and managing sessions. Therefore, on top of the servlet API, we have the JSP mechanism, which eases the writing of dynamic HTML pages a bit. Building sophisticated pages with a great deal of interactivity remains, however, a complex task, even with JSP available. Therefore, still another layer has been added, namely JSF, which is a standard for creating graphical components. Well... unfortunately writing JSF code is still no easy matter, thus there are wizards that generate part of this code ... and to benefit from Ajax[4] features, add to this the* ICEFaces *framework!*

Here again, obsolescence corresponds to a progressive phasing out of the low-level technologies in favor of these higher abstractions.

Just as for automation, nesting of concepts into abstraction essentially contributes to *vertical complexity*.

4.1.2.1. *Why complexity increases*

The exponential increase in resources and the correlated quick obsolescence of technologies have obviously directly benefited users in various ways: response times have decreased and graphical user interfaces have steadily become richer and slicker. Applications are moreover continuously scaling to accommodate ever-larger numbers of simultaneous users. Definitely, IT complexity has not been completely useless!

But on the other hand, let us face it; this seemingly limitless access to resources has also favored a kind of IT obesity and even IT anarchy. The reason for this is simple: as computing resources, CPU and RAM now appear essentially limitless to some developers, some of them tend to lose any sense of economy and sobriety in their designs.

---

4 Ajax is a web-development method to create highly interactive web pages that do not need to be reloaded completely when data are updated, thus providing a much smoother user experience.

As a consequence, the complexity of solutions has often grown totally out of proportion when considering the problems that had to be solved (or coded).

As an extreme example, consider an MDA tool to generate code for fetching a single row of data from a database. This code will most likely include calls to an O/R framework which, in turn, uses a large array of APIs whose code, in turn, runs on a virtual machine, which itself runs on top of a virtual operating system. The same result could be achieved by issuing an elementary, manually written, SQL request directly to the database!

Let us review the various other ways in which quick obsolescence generates growing heterogeneity and, hence, more complexity:

– First, the *time span* between successive versions of a given technology (say *Java EE 5* and *Java EE 6*) or between two equivalent technologies (say *Java* and *RubyJ*) *is usually too short to allow for a systematic and global update of all IT* within any company of significant size. Inevitably, the successive versions of a given technology and equivalent technologies will accumulate over the ages and progressively increase technological heterogeneity.

– A *thorough mastery of technologies by IT engineers often proves elusive*. Technologies are so numerous and change at such a fast pace that this prevents building a genuine technological expertise, not to mention a technological culture. A deep understanding of technology is, most often, practically impossible. True conceptual understanding and professional mastery is replaced by a sloppy, trial-and-error approach because there is just no other option.

Within the Java platform, the EJB technology (a specification for distributed business components), especially its first two versions, was notoriously so intricate that only few developers ever mastered it. Many even avoided using it altogether. The same seemed to happen more recently with JSF (a specification for building graphical components) and its various extensions. The lifecycle of these objects is so complex and subtle that many developers wonder whether learning this technology is really worthwhile and often prefer to stick with more straightforward solutions for which they at least gained some experience (e.g. Struts).

This remark is truer still for the tools supporting these APIs, which inherit their instability. Many tools, helpers, wizards, and templates were initially designed to enhance productivity but never had the opportunity to mature to become reliable and productive. Doing things the pedestrian way often proves faster.

In the worst case, which is unfortunately by no means uncommon, "freshman" developers use technologies, especially frameworks, without a clear understanding of their rationale. They use a framework mainly because it is already there, because some acronyms have reached the ears of deciders, or because some manager, who read the latest hype published in the IT press, has told them to do so.

The authors have several times met developers who used the Java Spring framework on a daily basis without knowing what dependency injection[5] is really good for!

---

5 Dependency injection is an OOP design pattern ensuring maximal decoupling of components and thus a high maintainability of software. Spring supplies the basic software infrastructure for just this.

The massive use of contract developers from software engineering companies makes this issue even more acute. Typically, these developers will face a new technological environment every 6 months or so, when they hop from one project to another. Their management expects them to adapt to their environment and to be quickly productive, which leaves little room for any deep understanding or professional mastery of anything. Hence, *forced dilettantism is the rule more often than not.*

Paraphrasing our earlier discussion on *simplicity through learning*, we can summarize the above remarks as the contrapositive statement: we observe *complexity through absence of understanding*.

– Closely related to the above is the *impossibility to make an educated choice among IT solutions* or tools. Quite often, solutions are roughly equivalent and pinpointing the subtle differences among a range of solutions would indeed require an effort that is beyond what most IT departments can afford. Under such circumstances, making rational choices becomes nearly impossible. The most common substitutes to reason are well-known: playing political games and/or practicing divination.

– Finally, and for the sake of completeness, let us recall the complexity that stems from the *illusion of limitless resources* that we mentioned earlier.

4.1.2.2. *Implementing simplicity*

Paralleling the previous remarks, let us see what simplicity has to offer:

– There is no obvious way to bypass the need to regularly *upgrade IT to new versions and standards*. Nevertheless, it is good to be aware that the SaaS[6] model now provides a new kind of solution for some applications and services. Recall

---

6 SaaS stands for Software as a Service.

that SaaS is an emerging model for buying and consuming computing resources. Rather than buying licenses for software packages from editors or designing custom software and running it in-house, the SaaS model proposes to buy ready-to-use services from a service provider. The provider is in charge of maintaining and scaling up the technical infrastructure that hosts the services, while customers have strictly no installation and no maintenance tasks under their responsibility. Currently, most applications and services which are likely to be migrated to the SaaS models are commodities. They include services like email, agendas, collaborative tools, backup tools, or tools for workflow management. Critical business applications remain for the moment in-house for obvious security reasons.

The prominent players in the SaaS marketplace are currently Google, Salesforce, Amazon, *and* Microsoft. *They mostly propose online office suites and an array of collaborative tools such as the Google Apps for instance. Business process management tools are available as well.*

There are also intermediate solutions between the classical in-house hosting and a full-fledged SaaS model. A provider can, for instance, propose a hosting infrastructure on which customers can run their applications. In this model, customers are basically just renting some quantity of CPU horsepower and some storage space. The maintenance of the hardware and all low-level IT services, such as web servers, is the responsibility of the provider, while the maintenance of middleware and applications is the responsibility of the customers. Still another possibility is that a provider offers a complete hosting platform, including application servers and databases.

> All these SaaS outsourcing variants are potential ways to mitigate uncontrolled complexity generated by IT obsolescence.

From the point of view of SaaS customers, this new kind of outsourcing is nothing but a specific form of *simplicity through hiding* complexity far away in the cloud!

– To *fight IT dilettantism* there is no miracle solution either. There are basically only two ways we can suggest. The first concerns the hiring process for IT professionals. The second concerns keeping proven IT professionals once they have been recognized.

Many job offers begin with a list of products and technologies the new employee is expected to master. Something like: the candidate must have working experience with: Java EE 6, PHP 5.3.5, MySQL 5.5.9, LIFERAY 6.0.5, JBoss AS 5 Development...

In other words, emphasis is wrongly placed on the most volatile kind of knowledge, namely knowledge of IT products, while more robust skills, such as conceptual thinking or deep knowledge of basic computing principles, are overlooked. And yet, basic knowledge would be the most valuable for developing intuitions on how to maintain a good balance between performance and maintainability in an IS. There is no deep mystery here. Filtering candidates on the basis of a list of products and then evaluating them on their degree of compliance with a given corporate culture requires fewer skills, from a recruiter, than evaluating a candidate's abilities at sound conceptual thinking.

A few years ago, one of the authors remembers the following joke that could be read on the signboards of the mathematics department in Princeton University.

"First rank people hire first rank people. Second rank people hire third rank people..." This slightly elitist joke, expressed using the metaphor of a mathematical sequence, illustrates quite well, we believe, what is really at stake in any serious recruitment process that is based on real skills...

Assuming these precious and rare skilled employees have been hired, they should now be kept for a long enough period to favor the emergence of a genuine enterprise tech culture. This namely entails encouraging longer technical careers (through the classical incentives) rather than encouraging everybody to become a manager or to shift to supposedly nobler business activities. Unfortunately, many IT departments now look more like a hodgepodge rather than structures dedicated to maintaining high levels of competence and intellectual integrity.

No doubt, some will consider this as a symptom of an overly idealistic worldview. We believe, however, that these remarks deserve at least to be meditated upon a little, because they are at the core of much of the nonsense in today's IT world. Referring once more to our simplicity principles, we summarize the above remarks in the following motto:

The IT organization and the hiring process should focus on making simplicity through learning at all possible.

– Let us address the *impossibility to make an educated choice among different IT solutions.* Our advice here is simple: avoid altogether any long and expensive comparative studies between tools or software packages. Experience shows that, most of the time, these solutions are by now nearly equivalent.

> What matters most is developing a true mastery and expertise of tools rather than the feature sets of these tools.

Favoring *simplicity through learning,* as advocated in the previous point, and systematically choosing the most standard and ubiquitous solutions, rather than the fanciest ones, is often your best bet. In the long run, knowing the details of the limitations of a product often proves more profitable than using fancy solutions that are only partly mastered. This is an example of *simplicity through reduction* (of the number of things to compare and to learn).

– One basic practice that is perhaps worth recalling to limit obsolescence is the following:

> Limit all specific development to business code. Do not attempt to reinvent the wheel by developing technical frameworks in-house.

Technical frameworks (*Spring, Hibernate, Struts,* MVC *implementations,* etc.) are sophisticated systems that require narrow specialization in algorithms and months of dedicated development. Such endeavors are way beyond what most IT departments can afford. Frameworks developed in-house will soon be totally outdated by more reliable products from the open-source community, and will only make heterogeneity worse.

– Complexity that is a consequence of the illusion of limitless resources was discussed earlier in sections 2.2.4 and 2.3.2. For convenience, we recall here what the main conclusion was:

> In many instances, encapsulating a lot of complexity can be traded for a moderate amount of learning.

4.1.3. *Absence of technological vision and leadership*

The last cause for growing heterogeneity we want to examine, after openness and rapid obsolescence of IT, is the absence of technological vision. Often, the absence of technological vision and leadership is itself a consequence of the fast pace at which IT evolves. Nevertheless, for the sake of clarity, we prefer here to consider it as a separate cause.

4.1.3.1. *Why complexity increases*

The context we have in mind here is the context where a *do-it-yourself* culture dominates the IT department. Developers, even beginners, are left without guidance and coordination; they are free to choose the technologies they like. In such circumstances, technology standards are often inexistent or, when they are available, they are not implemented as there is no authority to enforce them. IT choices are made opportunistically, project by project. Finally, there is no anticipation and problems are solved in a mostly reactive mode.

When tech gurus are in charge of making choices, they are often tempted to follow the latest hype, which they associate with a new playground.

A recent example of tech hype occurred in 2009–2010, when SharePoint, *was presented as an ambitious portal solution. Just one year later however, many customers realized they had been fooled by marketing. They are now looking for a better-adapted solution.*

This tech-hype situation is, however, increasingly rare.

Conversely, when managers with no IT background are making technological choices, they tend to favor short-term or purely political choices, without much consideration for building a sustainable IS.

When technology leadership is absent, the belief often develops that sophisticated project-management tools and processes can be a substitute for technical competence and responsibility. In other words, there is a "hide-behind-processes" kind of irresponsibility that develops, because making IT choices obviously requires both competence and responsibility! Let us face it: in many contexts, making decisions and assuming responsibilities does not actually favor climbing the professional ladder, especially if you are in a hurry.

> Processes are no substitute for technological competence and a sense of responsibility.

In the end, absence of technological vision only favors more heterogeneity and prevents the emergence of a genuine technical culture in the long run. Absence of technological leadership is especially harmful when coordination is required across several departments or business sectors.

As an example, implementing SOA architectures requires harmonizing a number of things such as: creating a shared model of business objects, defining a policy for versioning successive releases of services and setting up a mechanism for publishing new services in a shared directory. All of these need an system-architecture group that has that authority to make choices and to enforce them across all projects. Many SOA endeavors failed in recent years because of such a transverse coordinating structure was missing, not because of technological immaturity of web services standards.

Appendix 3 discusses more thoroughly the reasons for the failure of many service-oriented architecture (SOA) projects.

4.1.3.2. *Implementing simplicity*

Solutions for creating and maintaining a healthy tech culture are basically the same as those needed to prevent IT dilettantism, discussed in section 4.1.2. They concern the hiring process and incentive mechanisms. Promoting IT leadership implies acknowledging the importance of establishing a sound hierarchy within the IT department that is based primarily on technological competence and the ability to share it with others. Again, good processes will never be a substitute for the latter. *Simplicity through collective learning* is a stake here. It can only be developed in-house and therefore the use of external skills should be limited to the most specialized at tasks.

The overemphasis on processes amounts to confusing *simplicity through organization*, which is no doubt necessary, with *simplicity through learning*, that, let us emphasize it once more, has *no* substitute.

To promote long-term thinking, we should probably relate the incentives of IT management to long-term results rather than to the success of single projects, which notoriously encourages short-term thinking and narrow-mindedness. *Simplicity through time saving* should be evaluated on *significant* timescales, which exceed a single project's lifetime.

4.2. Changing requirements

For decades, delivering software that matches user's needs, on-time and within budget, has been the Holy Grail of the entire software industry. It is probably fair to say that, until now, this fundamental issue has not yet received a satisfactory answer. Moreover, things do not look really better in the foreseeable future. Unsurprisingly, we will not pretend here that we have solved this longstanding issue and hope our readers will not be too disappointed about it! In this section, we more modestly focus on the issue of producing software that meets user's requirements. We examine this question, keeping in mind the growth of complexity, which results when these requirements change over time.

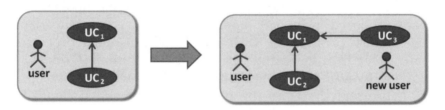

Figure 4.3. *Changing requirements, during the project and after an application has been developed, is a major source of uncontrolled complexity when they are not anticipated*

The problem with changing user requirements is twofold:

Applications must adapt to changing market conditions. This is true for functional requirements, that is new features are needed, as well as for non-functional requirements, that is, the application must scale to accommodate more users. Such changes usually occur over a period of several months or even years. We define *flexibility* as the ability to cope with such market-driven changes.

Specifications of applications change because they were not understood properly in the first place. This is more related to the difficulty in formalizing requirements in an unambiguous way. Changes of this nature occur over much shorter periods of time. They typically span the lifetime of a project. We define *agility* as the ability to cope with unclear requirements during the design of the system.

Numerous answers, both technical and organizational, have been proposed to address these fundamental issues. Before we review these answers, let us briefly describe the impact on value and let us examine why changing requirements increase complexity.

Impact on value

Flexibility, understood as the ability to adapt to changing market conditions, is quite straightforwardly related to *strategic value*. More precisely, it is related to maintaining a high strategic value when conditions will change in the future.

Flexibility will also help maintain user satisfaction when new features are needed. Again, flexibility will guarantee that *use value* remains high when conditions change. *Agility* is also, in some sense, related to user satisfaction, as this will guarantee their needs will really be taken into account starting with the design of applications.

Finally, *flexibility* is also, of course, an attribute of the *sustainability value*.

4.2.1. *Why complexity increases*

Quite generally, and beyond the present scope of just ISs, we should realize that tension is involved when we try to build systems that are both optimized and, at the same time, adaptable to changing requirements. The reason is simply because:

> Systems that are optimal are usually not flexible.

Totally optimized systems are usually *not* adaptable. There is thus a subtle balance to be found between optimization and adaptability, where the contribution of a system to innovation (which then strongly contributes to the strategic value) reaches its maximum. This line of thought was originally developed by a group of theoretical ecologists around Robert E. Ulanowicz and it was later applied to various domains, such as monetary crises, the Internet, and even civilizations. As far as we know, it has not been applied to IT yet, but it seems reasonable to speculate that ISs that fail to find this subtle balance point between optimization (of performance, of number of features) and adaptability (to varying demands) probably contain much unwanted complexity. We will not pursue this line of thought here, which would definitely require a deeper analysis and instead refer the interested reader to Ulanowicz's seminal work [ULA 09].

Coming back to our daily experience with IT, we can recognize two causes of growing complexity. Both follow as we acknowledge that *flexibility*, when needed, should be anticipated during software design:

– Uncontrolled complexity is generated when *flexibility appears to be needed but was not anticipated during design*.

Accommodating more flexibility then often turns out to be synonymous with increasing customization. The parameter space and data types that must be handled by the software become larger than initially expected. New exception handling mechanisms must be implemented to ensure that submitted data are valid and that its integrity is preserved when it is processed. Lack of anticipation most often translates into an unmanageable "combinatorial explosion" of cases that must be handled. Unanticipated new data types also require new conversion mechanisms that progressively accumulate until they get unmanageable. Then, all of these in turn introduce unpredictability into the system.

– Needless complexity is also generated, in a more insidious way, when *flexibility was wrongly anticipated while it was actually not needed*! Implementing flexibility definitely requires additional design effort and more abstraction layers. When flexibility was not needed, this work is useless and, worse, the layers of abstractions that were created lead to software whose complexity is incommensurate with its original purpose. Such situations have occurred frequently in recent years, partly because of extensive hype around SOA and flexibility, which both became almost an IT dogma (see Appendix 3 for a more detailed analysis).

We can tie in here with the analysis provided in the alignment trap paper that we mentioned in section 3.3.3 by making the following identification:

> Companies which attempt to achieve flexibility in their business processes before they have even identified stable components and a stable business semantic are precisely those which are stuck in the alignment trap.

Finally, let us come to the complexity stemming from the need for *agility*. Recall that agility refers to coping with unclear or incomplete requirements while software is being designed. In this case, complexity is generated when it is not acknowledged that classical, linear project planning is not suitable anymore.

Later, we shall review the technical and organizational answers that have been traditionally given to these agility and flexibility issues and interpret them as simplicity principles.

4.2.2. *Implementing simplicity*

4.2.2.1. *Technical answers*

Technical answers primarily address the flexibility issue. Basically, there is just one useful idea that helps cope with changing requirements, namely identify things that do *not* change![7] Roughly speaking, changing requirements can be addressed by recombining existing, stable components with minimal additional design.

This is the *idea of reuse* that we shall now examine. There are many different kinds of reuses that can be useful in shaping a flexible IS. We will classify them according to the layer of the IS architecture where they occur.

4.2.2.1.1. Reuse in software architecture

At this level, reuse takes the form of libraries and frameworks that encapsulate expert knowledge in design patterns and algorithm implementation. More explicitly, this form of reuse implies some pieces of code being used several times in different places.

---

7 Incidentally, it is interesting to note that physicists, who are interested in dynamics of physical systems, use exactly the same strategy; they first look for constants of motions that are consequences of sets of symmetries.

The Spring framework *for instance, which implements the IoC design pattern, can be reused several times in different business applications.*

This kind of reuse occurs at the design stage. In a sense, it is a static form of reuse. It is an application of *simplicity through hiding* (encapsulation of expert knowledge) and of *simplicity through reduction* (the same solution is factorized to be used in many places).

Promoting systematic reuse of this kind is the responsibility of a global architecture team that should be granted sufficient authority by the CIO to actually enforce a clear set of rules.

4.2.2.1.2. Reuse in functional architecture

It is not uncommon that different business applications have to use the same services. They all need an authentication service, for example. The authentication service, in turn, works with a corporate directory of users, which is also used to define access rights for business applications. Services that manage lists of customers or products, as well as billing services, are also profitably shared.

When these kinds of services are shared, we speak of reuse at the application-architecture level. The most advanced form of this type of reuse is actually described by SOA principles, which have received a lot of attention in recent years. Yet, blind application of these SOA principles has led to much disillusionment. We defer critical examination of SOA architectures to Appendix 3 because this requires the introduction of a new concept, the operating model of a company, which would be somewhat off-topic here.

When looking for stable elements in an IS, we should also look for stable data, stable business rules, and stable business processes. Identifying and managing referential data in a company is the subject called MDM[8]. Master data are opposed to transactional data because this is usually managed using different policies and different tools.

The IS Rating Tool promoted by Pierre Bonnet [BON 11] is a framework that aims to measure what he defines as the intrinsic value of an IS. *The basic idea is to rate the knowledge, the governance and technical quality of these three types of repositories: MDM, business rules and business process repositories[9]. For this he enumerates an extensive list of measurement points.*

4.2.2.1.3. Reuse on the semantic level

This is perhaps a less familiar form of reuse. It is especially useful when setting up SOA architecture, which requires defining a pivot format for data handled by the services. Such a format defines the semantics and syntax of data that are shared among the services. For larger companies, the business vocabulary to be formalized can include hundreds of entities. Experience shows that the task of organizing such a large number of concepts in a coherent whole is often beyond what even the largest IT department can afford. Establishing such *reusable models of entities and processes* is really an R&D task that must be organized

---

8 MDM = Master Data Management is a set of methods that consistently define and manage the non-transactional data entities of an organization.
9 A thorough presentation of Pierre Bonnet's ideas is given in his book [BON 11]. A detailed table of content is available at: http://www. sustainableitarchitecture.com/bookisrating.html.

at the level of an industry: banking, insurance, car industry, pharmacy, railroad industry, telecommunications, and so on.

The eTOM[10] is such a model that defines the most widely used and accepted standard for business processes in the telecommunications industry. It is probably not just by chance that one of the fastest-moving industries was also one of the first to promote this new form of capitalization.

Whenever such semantic models exist, they should be used, even if this implies extending it to match a company's specificities. We believe there is a huge source of savings in using this type of industry-wide business object and/or process models. Unfortunately, the potential of this type of semantic and syntax capitalization has not yet been widely acknowledged. The reason is probably that companies that own such a model consider it as a hard-won competitive advantage that they are not eager to share.

To conclude this section on flexibility, note that there is actually a close parallel with section 4.1.2, namely:

Changes in technologies are best addressed by emphasizing what is stable in computing: basic concepts, patterns, and intuition on balancing performance with maintainability.

Changes in requirements are best addressed by emphasizing what is stable in the IS: software components and the semantic of business objects and processes.

> The best way to cope with change is to clearly identify what is stable.

---

10 eTOM = enhanced Telecom Operations Map.

4.2.2.2. *Organizational answers*

Organizational answers address the need for agility during design time. They can also help identify situations in which building flexibility can be avoided, when writing quick-and-dirty throwaway code turns out to be the best solution. As these solutions are only loosely related to our simplicity principles, we list them here for the sake of completeness and coherence, but we will not go into any details.

4.2.2.2.1. Achieving agility

Many project-management methods were designed in the last years to achieve agility in software design: RUP[11], XP[12], and Scrum[13], just to name a few. Countless books have been written on the subject, but they more or less all share a common set of features or best practices:

– They are *iterative and incremental,* meaning that software is designed in steps rather than planned in advance. It is fair to say that the implementation of an iterative process needs dedicated tools for performing continuous integration (Maven, Ant, etc.) of the project. The answer to agility is thus partly technical as well.

– They *involve the users* much more than more traditional project-management methods. In a sense, they all acknowledge that customers do not precisely know what they want at the beginning of a project and that they often will change their minds. Each increment or partial release of the system is meant to provoke remarks from customers, which in turn will provide a better understanding of what their needs really are.

---

11 RUP = Rational Unified Process is a process created by the Rational Software Corporation, now acquired by IBM. It is based on UP (Unified Process in complement to the UML language).

12 XP = Extreme Programming advocates frequent releases and strong collaboration with customers.

13 Scrum is not an acronym for anything!

Loosely speaking, these best practices can be related to *simplicity through learning,* because they all assume that learning what the users want is essential and that this takes an incompressible amount of time. XP explicitly advocates building a system in the simplest possible way but with no further guidance as to what exactly simplicity means.

Using continuous-integration tools is an instance of *simplicity through hiding*: low-level tasks of building the systems are handled by automations because humans are far too error-prone for such recurrent, low-level tasks.

Collective code ownership, promoted by XP, means that responsibility is shared among all developers in a team. One XP practice explicitly requires each developer to consider his colleagues as equally competent to change the code when this is required. Thus, we have an instance of *simplicity through trust*.

4.2.2.2.2. Deciding when writing throwaway code is the best option?

There are indeed cases when writing throwaway code turns out to be the best solution. There are no strict rules to follow here, as this will depend mostly on the expected duration of a piece of code and the likeliness of its future reuse. Nevertheless, a little classification of applications can probably help in making this decision:

– On the one hand, we have *critical business applications* for business users. These are usually complex systems, which will probably require change over time when market opportunities vary but which are stable enough to consider building sustainable software.

– On the other hand, we have *applications for customers*, which depend on much more haphazard events. For reasons of image or immediate competitiveness, it may be preferable for these applications to use the latest technologies, without worrying too much about sustainability.

In the finance sector, there are many situations that can warrant producing quick-and-dirty code. Portfolio managers, for instance, often quickly need some new service, which will help them perform risk or profitability analysis and will be used only for a very limited period of time.

These are good candidates for throwaway code.

Proponents of agile methods (see *Lean Software Development*, discussed in section 2.2) usually consider that emphasizing flexibility too much is a mistake. They claim that the amount of capitalization work involved to achieve flexibility is unrealistically large. We consider such a point of view as excessive and prefer to distinguish two categories of applications above: one deserves capitalization, while the other does not.

4.3. Human factors

From the beginning, we emphasized that evaluating the complexity or the value(s) of an IS is a difficult and ambiguous task, because the technical aspects of IT are deeply entangled with human factors. By human factors, we mean such diverse elements as: team coordination, commitment management, lifelong learning of technologies, or relations with customers. The range of social and cognitive skills that plays a significant role in shaping the evolution of an IS is broad. Analyzing them could probably warrant a book in itself. For this reason, we will not seek completeness here, but rather focus on a limited number of topics, which play a clear role regarding complexity issues. We restrict ourselves to human factors directly witnessed in the course of IT projects with which we were involved as IT consultants. Some of the issues addressed here will partly overlap those that we discussed earlier. Nevertheless, we consider it useful to look at these anew, this time from a more social and cognitive perspective.

Multidisciplinarity   Demotivation   Local interest is not global interest

Figure 4.4. *Three important human factors that can significantly contribute to an uncontrolled increase in complexity: multidisciplinarity of skills, demotivation of individuals, and the fact that optimizing the global interest is usually different than local interest*

The impact on value of these human factors will be discussed separately in sections 4.3.1–4.3.3.

4.3.1. *Multidisciplinarity*

4.3.1.1. *Why complexity increases*

The task of building and maintaining an IS in operational conditions requires that many different skills collaborate, probably more than in most other professions. Uncontrolled complexity can result as a consequence of the many ambiguities and misunderstandings that occur when these people with different skills, vocabulary, and backgrounds must exchange information. Moreover, individuals, especially IT specialists, are commonly expected to master many different technologies. When this number of technologies grows too large, it will promote dilettantism, which in turn will favor disorder and unpredictability.

As an extreme example, consider the skills expected from a good IT project manager. *He/she needs to communicate with three different kinds of stakeholders with very different backgrounds:*

– The development team, *in charge of implementing the project. As a leader, the project manager is expected to understand at least the basics of the technologies that will be used in the project. This is necessary to be able to make sound decisions and arbitrate among various IT solutions. A good technical background will also contribute to his/her credibility with the team.*

– The business management, *which has mandated the implementation of the system. As a privileged interlocutor of the business management, the project manager should be able to grasp the basic ins and outs of the business processes and also master the associated business vocabulary.*

– The CFO *who is responsible for controlling costs and making sure that the project stays within budget. The project manager will need to negotiate with him/her any possible budget overrun.*

In the end, the IT project manager will have to decide what is technically feasible or not under the given constraints of time, skills and budget.

The role of IT project manager is probably the extreme example of the need for multiple competences and for the ability to communicate on different levels. While most other stakeholders can (and often do) hide behind specialization in an attempt to limit their responsibilities (to technical, financial, or organizational matters), the IT project manager is exposed to the technical, organizational, and financial fronts simultaneously. Ideally, he or she is an IT specialist and a diplomatic negotiation expert. This is a tall order for a single individual.

Even within IT, the range of skills needed in an average project is usually quite large: developers, for instance, need to master many programming languages and IDEs[14] and integration tools. This is related to what we termed the *horizontal complexity* in section 4.1.

> A high horizontal complexity increases the number of technologies that each IT specialist should master.

Vertical complexity, which we recall is related to the different levels of abstraction present in an IS, is somewhat different.

> A high vertical complexity increases the need for specialists in different IT skills to exchange information and knowledge across their domain of expertise.

As language and vocabulary usually depend on the domain of expertise, this raises the chances for ambiguities or misunderstanding.

When a business specialist refers to a "business object", a developer might quickly associate this concept with an OOP "class", while a relational database specialist will associate it to a "table" in a schema with a primary and foreign key. Although similar, these concepts are different and cannot be confused.

---

14 IDE = Integrated Development Environment.

When many different skills are needed to accomplish a task, their respective specialists will first need to learn how to understand each other.

4.3.1.2. *Implementing simplicity*

Let us quickly recall the possible way to mitigate the above issues:

– *Responsibilities* should be shared among all stakeholders. Situations in which a single role (as the project manager described above) assumes most of the responsibilities should be avoided (*simplicity through trust...* that everybody will assume part of the responsibilities).

– *Horizontal complexity* is mitigated by defining and enforcing technological standards and avoiding a generalized DIY culture (*simplicity through reduction...* of the number of technologies).

– *Vertical complexity* is mitigated by:

- limiting the number of levels of abstraction in the architecture (*simplicity through reduction*). Recall that this was discussed in depth in the subsection "Good abstraction is a form of simplicity!" under section 2.3.2.

- requiring each IT or business-process specialist to learn the basics of the vocabulary and concepts of his or her co-workers (*simplicity through learning*).

Everyone should learn part of others' jobs!

- promoting, in the long run, a uniform and companywide communication culture, based on a consistent use of standard notations such as UML and BPMN.

- incentives that exist to favor communication and sharing skill at least as much as developing advanced technical skills.

Impact on value

Perhaps the most direct relation of multidisciplinarity to value is regarding *use value*. Understanding users' needs, being able to precisely document them, and to see what is reasonably feasible or not requires people with technical skills and with a deep understanding of the business processes, to see how these could benefit from IT.

On the purely technical side, limiting software complexity (horizontal and vertical) via the simplicity principles above can only improve the *sustainability value*.

4.3.2. *Disempowerment of IT Skills*

4.3.2.1. *Why complexity increases*

There is a vicious circle that generates complexity, which is somewhat implicit in several of our earlier remarks. Let us state it more explicitly here. Consider an IS with a large overall vertical complexity (i.e. many nested abstraction levels or scales) and also a large K-complexity in most of its architecture layers (i.e. models are extensive and detailed). This complexity (see section 2.1.5) makes it difficult for stakeholders to build a coherent mental overview of the system as whole. Under such circumstances, decisions regarding technical or functional changes in the IS are made in partial blindness. Nobody, even within the IT department, has a clear idea of the interdependence of the various components and chances for spotting reuse opportunities are often lost. As a result, needless complexity and randomness can only increase further. End of loop!

Being aware of this vicious circle, we could imagine that the final solution would be maintaining a consistent multiscale set of models for the whole system. The hardware infrastructure, the application architecture, the software architecture, the physical deployment, the business processes, and so on should have an up-to-date model and these should be available companywide. But actually, even this would not suffice because the lack of a global overview has a deeper and more insidious cause, namely the demotivation and disempowerment of IT stakeholders that result from a biased idea of rationalization. The point is that building an overall view of a complex system requires an incompressible amount of intellectual effort to which only self-motivated individuals will consent. No matter how much modeling is done, it will not help much if this basic motivation is absent from a majority of IT stakeholders. We are, here, at the true junction of technical and human issues.

> Mastering complexity, in the end, can only be accomplished by self-motivated individuals.

As inelegant as it may sound, *proletarianization*[15] is the term that captures best what we have in mind. This term has traditionally been associated with the working class, where it refers to people who are progressively disempowered because their initial expertise has been replaced by machines as a consequence of a rationalization effort. As the pressure for rationalization only increases, the computer industry is now facing proletarianization as well and it does so at all levels of responsibility:

Business users now see more and more of their original tasks being automated in software packages. Parts of their

---

15 The concept of proletarianization has been recently promoted by Ars industrialis, an international association created and led by French philosopher Bernard Stiegler, who advocates a "new industrial policy for mind technologies", see http://arsindustrialis.org/.

expertise and their creativity are considered obsolete and counterproductive.

IT users and developers use an increasing number of tools to automate low-level tasks. Continuous-integration tools, mentioned earlier, now perform sophisticated deployment tasks on clustered architectures. IDEs offer wizards to quickly set up the skeleton of applications. Software frameworks encapsulate sophisticated algorithms and pattern implementations. Thus, progressively, low-level workings are hidden. The danger is that this basic knowledge also gets progressively lost, and with it the intuition that is necessary to achieve the subtle balance between performance and maintainability. Yet, this intuition remains essential for designing sustainable systems.

System administrators of mail systems, databases, and enterprise directories could disappear from many IT departments, as the SaaS model is spreading, see section 4.1.2.

These examples are really different instances of complexity encapsulation, respectively: encapsulation of business procedures, of IT tasks, and of administration tasks. Recall that in section 2.2.2, we identified hiding complexity as one form of simplicity. However, we have also seen that the concept of simplicity is indeed much richer than just hiding complexity, hence our definition of simplicity is a combination of six different aspects. As a consequence, mitigating complexity cannot be achieved naively by just maximizing hiding.

An excessive faith in the possibility to encapsulate any kind of complexity can lead to disempowerment and loss of motivation.

Let us come more explicitly to the relationship of proletarianization to uncontrolled complexity. Proletarianization, understood as an excess of complexity encapsulation and standardization, encourages excessive specialization of skills. This overspecialization conflicts in turn with the ability to build a coherent mental picture of a complex system, which is essential to maintaining it in operational condition in the long run.

In IT departments, it is thus not uncommon to see people, especially young and inexperienced developers, being overwhelmed by the vertical complexity of their IT environment. Indeed, there are tens of APIs to master, the IDE, the various continuous-integration tools, the entanglement of frameworks, not to mention the intricacies of business processes, and so on. In these situations, when expert advice is unavailable to provide guidance through the local tech-jungle, many people spontaneously develop some immunity to nonsense: they simply let their critical thinking atrophy and accept acting in absurd ways.

Modern IDEs all offer sophisticated debugging tools that efficiently allow pinpointing errors and exceptions in code, by setting conditional break points, or by running code stepwise and investigating the content of variables. We have often met younger developers who avoided using such debugging tools altogether and preferred to go the old-fashioned way, namely by painstakingly writing explicit messages to the console. The explanation is simple: being overwhelmed with tens of tools, APIs and frameworks, they gave up even with the basic task of setting up and mastering their daily work environment.

Demotivated people end up concluding that "there is no serious hope in such a technical and organizational mess". Getting used to nonsense eventually appears as the most reasonable and the least painful way to survive. In other words, proletarianization can eventually destroy the meaning of any kind of human activity. With critical thinking gone, so will any sense of initiative and any sense of responsibility.

> Pushed to its logical limit, proletarianization amounts to considering people as simple resources, on the same footing as machines. Human minds end up behaving like machines, only in a less reliable way.

The example of the demotivated developer mentioned above is probably extreme but proletarianization definitely exists at different degrees in most IT departments. It could even gain momentum in the near future with the advent of the SaaS model that will inevitably redistribute responsibilities within IT organizations.

4.3.2.2. *Implementing simplicity*

Sociological studies[16] have proven, time and again, that the classical economic incentives are not appropriate to developing the kind of motivation that is needed to master complex systems. Unfortunately, it looks like this well-established scientific fact has not yet made its way through much of the corporate environment.

Thus, the first step in implementing simplicity, against proletarianization, is perhaps acknowledging the following:

---

16 See, for example, career analyst Dan Pink on the "science of motivation" and references therein: http://www.ted.com/talks/dan_pink_on_motivation.html.

Proletarianization is the result of a simple mistake: forgetting about the specifics of the human brain, whose primary fuel, to work properly on complex systems, is to work on things that seem to make sense.

The opposite of proletarianization within an IT department is unfortunately difficult to characterize. There is nevertheless a concrete working model for it, which is provided by the open-source software (OSS) community. The OSS community has achieved a tremendous amount of high-quality work, realizing software infrastructure that still underlies much of the modern web: *Linux OS*, *Apache* web server, *MySQL* database, *Hibernate* O/R framework, to name just a few. The point here is that all of these have been achieved using values and incentives that connect directly with self-motivation: working on things that make sense (because they are widely used), creating and sharing knowledge, and being recognized by peers[17].

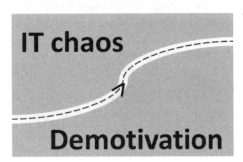

Figure 4.5. *The fine line between IT chaos and demotivation*

There is certainly no easy and obvious answer for implementing such a *contribution economy*, locally, within an

---

17 This is, by the way, also the primary incentive within the scientific community.

IT department. Nevertheless, keeping the OSS community in mind, as a living example of collective efficiency, cannot hurt.

The core of the difficulty lies in avoiding the following two antagonistic pitfalls:

– *Avoiding proletarianization* implies setting up a contributive organization where individuals can take initiatives and be creative. This will promote individual responsibility and personal involvement. The "Empower the team" principle in the *Lean Software Development* addresses precisely this issue of proletarianization by asking managers to first listen to the developers, rather than the other way around, so that their suggestions will be better targeted. The idea is also to hire people who have enough autonomy to get the job done without requiring extensive management.

– Avoiding IT chaos implies setting up an organization from which generalized DIY is banished and where standards are defined and enforced. Recall that this aspect of things was discussed extensively in section 4.1.3.

The fine line lies in between and the only way the above assertions can be non-contradictory is for different rules to apply to different IT populations.

We conclude this section on disempowerment with the following summary:

> This book is best considered as an invitation to deproletarizing IT. In other words, we claim that it is a good idea to stop believing that everything in IT can be encapsulated in rules, algorithms and templates. Many of the trickiest complexity issues are indeed caused by a progressive loss of both common sense and a few simplicity intuitions.

Impact on value

Fighting disempowerment will clearly contribute to the *sustainability value*, which is strongly dependent on IT skills being able to respond to unforeseen technical changes in a creative way.

In specific cases, excessive automation of business processes can also prevent creative answers to changing market opportunities that can only be addressed with imagination and creativity. In this sense, it is related to *strategic value* as well.

4.3.3. *Local interest is not global interest*

4.3.3.1. *Why complexity increases*

Finding the best strategy to maximize global interest versus individual interest is a generic social issue that is faced by all human groups, whatever their size is: countries, tribes, companies, and IT departments are, of course, no exception. As clearly neither politics nor sociology is the core subject of this book, we shall limit ourselves to a few simple remarks, which summarize situations that we have repeatedly witnessed on IT projects and that pertain directly to complexity.

The two common ways in which individual interest differs from global interest are the "resistance to change" syndrome, on the one hand, and the "playground syndrome", on the other:

– The former attitude, *conservatism*, is the most natural way to react for individuals who have adapted to an existing situation and who perceive changes mainly as a threat to their privileges, comfort, or influence. Changes in IT are by no means neutral, because they often induce a redistribution of responsibilities. When an organization changes, as for instance with the advent of SaaS, this can obviate the need for some specific expertise that is now outsourced. Similarly, a younger generation sometimes has new skills that the previous generation did not bother to acquire.

> *When Java emerged, ten years ago, as a generic platform for enterprise computing, tension was often observed between the "old" COBOL mainframe experts and the younger OOP generation.*

Complexity then accumulates as a consequence of this inertia:

> Simple or simpler solutions are not implemented, for fear of disturbing some influential stakeholders in their beloved habits.

– At the other extreme of the psychological spectrum, we find the *tech-hype*, which pushes some minds to believe that the latest technologies are necessarily faster, better, or more reliable. Changing technology or tools, for them, is a matter for rejoicing. A new playground just opened and not trying it is just not an option for them. Complexity then accumulates as a consequence of the quick obsolescence of most of these one-day-hype technologies, as we discussed in section 4.1.3.

Sadly, patterns in which personal interest differs from global interest are nearly infinite.

Performing capitalization of IT expertise, which is really *simplicity through collective learning* applied, often requires substantial orderliness as this implies additional work once a project is finished. This is not always perceived as useful for the individual who is in charge and thus serves as yet another example where a company's interest and individual interests do not obviously coincide.

Besides the aforementioned examples, there are also many cases in which global interest is forgotten altogether because a group of stakeholders believe that they have an interest in the *failure* of some projects. In the tense psychological and political situations that characterize many IT departments, these motivations for failure can actually become the dominant force of the evolution of an IS, whether the management acknowledges this or not. Chaos is then not very far away.

4.3.3.2. *Implementing simplicity*

There are few general solutions that we are aware of to address these issues. Two of them may be trivial-sounding but are still worth mentioning:

– The first is to imagine a set of incentives to align, as much as possible, individual and global interests. Apart from traditional incentives, the best solution within an IT department is to *use technology in a more contributive way*, as discussed in section 4.3.2. This can imply performing technology intelligence, publishing expert information on corporate blogs and seminars, realizing prototypes, or getting involved in training for beginners. Maintaining tech-enthusiasm and professional self-esteem at healthy levels is certainly a good option to align individual and global interests.

– Second, as this is a non-ideal world, *it should be acknowledged that it is simply impossible to always match local or personal interest with the global, companywide interest.*

Consider the aim of achieving companywide flexibility in business processes, say, to maximize the strategic value of the IS. Most of the time, this goal will require defining companywide standards regarding how processes are executed. Defining reusable services typically also often involves defining new integrated data structures. These tasks will often disrupt the local decision processes and the habits within the various local business units. The local management may lose part of its autonomy in favor of the company management. Moreover, some local processes or data structures, that were considered perfectly efficient so far, may need to be replaced with less efficient ones only to comply with the companywide standards.

It thus looks important to acknowledge the following fact of life:

> Achieving companywide flexibility can require decreasing the flexibility of local processes and the local decision autonomy.

Increasing global flexibility usually involves a stage where local flexibility first decreases. It is during this transitory period that global and local interests do not coincide. Such changes, of course, do not happen overnight. We can consider it as still another illustration that *simplicity through learning* definitely needs time.

Impact on value

There is no obvious preferred link to any of the three concepts of values here, as global interest could increase any of these. If we consider, however, that achieving companywide flexibility (as opposed to local flexibility) is *the* main goal of IT, then the link will more naturally be to the *strategic value*.

Chapter 5

Simplicity Best Practices

In seeking the unattainable, simplicity only gets in the way.
Alan Jay Perlis – Epigrams on Programming

5.1. Putting simplicity principles into practice

In the previous chapter, we categorized the various sources of uncontrolled increase of complexity for information systems and also discussed how general simplicity principles could favor creation of value. Now, to turn these principles into a more practical framework, we first describe a *generic information system* in terms of architecture layers, applications, and physical and logical dependencies. For each of the architecture layer, we then suggest concrete simplicity measures to mitigate the three main sources of unwanted complexity, namely growing technical heterogeneity, changing requirements, and the selection of human factors we decided to consider.

5.2. Defining a generic IS

The diversity of ISs is obviously huge and this makes it rather hard to define a sensible generic architecture. We thus prefer to take the point of view of IS architects here and define three standard architecture levels:

The physical architecture: This includes infrastructure components such as hardware, network, security tools, archiving tools, and administration and monitoring tools that underlie an IS.

The software architecture: This includes, broadly speaking, any piece of code, modules, libraries, and frameworks that are used in the applications that are part of the IS. We further distinguish three sub-layers in the software architecture that are commonly referred to in three-tiered architectures.

– *Data-access layer:* This includes all code that directly manages data, irrespective of the format: relational databases, XML files, or flat files. This code might be written by hand or might be generated. This layer also includes all O/R code when OOP languages are used.

– *Service layer:* This layer includes both technical and business services. Technical services, for instance, are in charge of providing an access to resources such as databases, to CICS[1] transaction servers, document generators, mail services, or LDAP directories. Business services also provide a coherent view of business data such as customers and suppliers. They can either implement business rules or coordinate the invocation of other business services. Business services can rely on technical services.

– *User interface:* This layer includes all code that supports the graphical user interface, whether it is a web interface or a rich client for stand-alone applications. It

---

1 CICS stands for Customer Information Control System. It is a transaction server that runs on IBM mainframes.

also includes portal technologies that aggregate various information sources.

The functional architecture: This covers the features of the IS essentially as they appear in functional specifications. If UML notation is used, this would include all *Use Case diagrams*, together with *Sequence Diagrams* and *Activity Diagrams* that complement them. Managing a customer contract or tracking of product shipping are examples of such Use Cases.

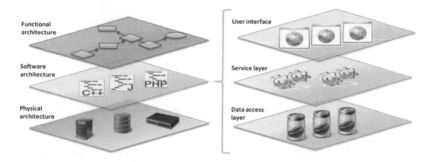

Figure 5.1. *The three architecture levels to which we can apply simplicity actions: functional architecture, software architecture, physical architecture. The Software architecture is subdivided, in turn, into the usual three tiers: the user interface, the service layer, and the data access layer*

An application in the IS usually spans these three layers, in the sense that it has relevant descriptions in each of them. Especially important for our complexity considerations are the dependences between *applications*. There can be a *physical dependence* between two applications, which means that they explicitly exchange data at one or more architectural levels. There can also be a *logical dependence*, which means that data from one application may be used indirectly as input to another, in a business process that is not entirely automated.

5.3. A simplicity framework

This section should be regarded as a best-practice guide. It is not necessarily meant to be read in sequence. The table below lists some key aspects in generating complexity within the different architecture layers; the items refer to topics covered in detail in the next five subsections.

	Growing technical heterogeneity	Changing requirements	Human factors
Hardware (section 5.3.1)	Different OSs and middleware often contribute to high heterogeneity	Recurrent demands from IT people should be streamlined	Large-scale use of SaaS could bring disempowerment in the near future
Software – Data Access (section 5.3.2)	Many APIs and frameworks made available in recent years	Changing data structures is notoriously complex and costly	Excessive trust in code generation creates needless complexity
Software – Services (section 5.3.3)	Numerous physical dependences requires many protocol conversions	Changes in functional requirements impact business services first	Specialized skills and creativity are important
Software – User Interface (section 5.3.4)	User-interface technologies abound	User-interface requirements change particularly fast	Technology is often used as a playground
Functional Architecture (section 5.3.5)	Diversity of tools and modeling notation	Logical inconsistencies may result from constant changes	Excessive automation of business processes should be avoided

The next five subsections are organized as follows: for each of the above five architecture layers or sub-layers, we discuss the specifics of three main causes of complexity. We then discuss how this complexity can be evaluated and mitigated using simplicity actions.

5.3.1. *Simplicity in hardware*

In this section, we analyze how the growing of complexity in the hardware layer can be mitigated. The perspective is that of IT production teams, whose responsibility is operating and maintaining the hardware in operational conditions. IT production and hardware accumulate most of the complexity factors that we identified in the last chapter and therefore make an appropriate starting point for describing a simplicity framework.

5.3.1.1. *Growing technical heterogeneity*

Heterogeneity can be quite pronounced in IT production departments and it is not uncommon that large IT departments still have mainframe AS/400 systems running in parallel with Windows and UNIX systems. For the sake of simplicity, we conventionally include the operating system when describing hardware.

Technical heterogeneity is often a consequence of the emergency mode in which much of the work is done: "Just get the darn thing working!" is the response. As a matter of fact, emergency often supersedes compliance with predefined standards and rules. Finding elegant solutions and using the latest technologies is considered even less important. In IT production departments, pragmatism is often pushed to its extreme and, once things run smoothly, the motto is: "Don't touch it!" Under such circumstances, provisional solutions and patches will accumulate without anybody in particular worrying about the overall coherence and homogeneity of the system. As the vision of the mutual dependences among the different pieces of hardware is progressively lost, reliability inevitably deteriorates.

When two companies and their respective IT departments merge, the heterogeneity can even increase in dramatic or unmanageable proportions.

5.3.1.1.1. Evaluation

Evaluating the heterogeneity of hardware should take into account both the diversity of systems and their age. Older technologies should certainly be penalized more than recent technologies.

A quick evaluation of the CAPEX and the OPEX[2] can help determine whether moving to a new technology will prove profitable. This will provide an opportunity not only to mitigate heterogeneity, but also to help decrease maintenance costs.

5.3.1.1.2. Simplicity actions

As an application of the *simplicity by reduction* principle, the blueprint of each company should clearly define a default operating system for new systems and define clear rules for possible exceptions.

Applying the SaaS model, wherever it makes sense, is probably the best option for reducing technical homogeneity in hardware by suppressing it altogether. This is still another application of *simplicity by hiding,* as the hardware is actually not "suppressed" but only transferred to the service provider. The decision to move to the SaaS model should not be taken lightly, though. Facilities-management tasks should be taken into account, as well as how much loss in IT skills the SaaS model might induce (see section 5.3.1.3).

---

2 CAPEX = capital expenditures are expenditures creating future benefits.
OPEX = operating expenditure is an ongoing cost for a system.

Replacing all equipment to homogenize technologies is rarely a realistic option. A specific form of *simplicity through hiding and abstraction* that can be applied here is virtualization[3].

5.3.1.2. *Changing requirements*

Hardware is relatively stable in the long run and stays largely unaffected by changing requirements, at least when compared with software architecture, which changes on much shorter timescales.

5.3.1.2.1. Evaluation

Try to determine the proportion of recurrent requests, from internal customers (IT users, developers, etc.), whose fulfillment would better be addressed using more formal processes.

5.3.1.2.2. Simplicity actions

To face changing requirements using *simplicity by reduction*, a good solution for IT production is to provide a catalogue of solutions to their internal "customers" (research department, etc.). This restricted set of solutions should then be streamlined.

5.3.1.3. *Human factors*

IT operations are traditionally subdivided into many specialized tasks and thus, quite naturally, face a *multidisciplinarity* issue. These usually do not require much creativity or deep understanding of IT, though. Experience shows problems occur mainly because of a lack of communication between specialists than because of language ambiguities.

---

3 Virtualization is the creation of a virtual version of some computing resource, such as an operating system, a server, a storage device, and network resources.

While IT operations can certainly appear quite inflexible at times to project teams, they are, by contrast, very flexible internally. The risk of *proletarianization* is thus not really significant, as IT-operation tasks remain largely craft. The advent of the SaaS model could, however, change things in the near future. Clearly, some knowledge (administration of servers, databases, etc.) will appear more and more useless in this new context. Due to its uselessness, this knowledge could then progressively be lost. This could later prove penalizing when that knowledge will actually be required. Some vigilance will also be required to make sure that the SaaS model will not destroy IT teams' sense of responsibility by offering them the possibility to blame SaaS providers for all performance and availability issues.

IT operations people are often in close connection with business management and they are the ones who are woken up at night when something goes wrong. Their interests thus coincide rather naturally with the global interest of the company.

5.3.1.3.1. Evaluation

One obvious metric to use, to evaluate multidisciplinarity, is to count the number of people or skills necessary to solve each kind of issue.

5.3.1.3.2. Simplicity actions

One solution is to provide training to improve the diversity of skills mastered by each team member, which will thus decrease the number of people involved in solving a problem.

5.3.2. *Simplicity in software – data access*

5.3.2.1. *Growing technical heterogeneity*

Languages and tools for handling data are countless in this layer and they largely contribute to the horizontal complexity when no technological leadership is available and when no clear standards have been enacted. It is fair to say that this layer currently often remains quite anarchic. Over the last 10 years, technologies or APIs have appeared at such a fast pace that the former version could rarely be fully mastered before the next version arrived. Obsolescence, thus, has been relatively important, even if probably not as quick as in the user-interface layer. Some tools, such as ETL[4], can also favor an increasing heterogeneity as they allow conversion from one format to another, thus delaying the painstaking task of designing more consistent data models.

5.3.2.1.1. Evaluation

Taking inventory of the number of technologies, languages, and tools is a first step. Most of the time, this comes down to mapping out existing data structures, protocols, and libraries.

The quality and availability of technical documentation will also provide a good insight into the maturity of the data-access layer. If standards have been defined at all, one should evaluate how well they are enforced on each new project.

5.3.2.1.2. Simplicity actions

The first measure is to define and enforce a set of consistent standards that will apply to any new project. The responsibility for this should be assigned to a global team in charge of defining data structures. More precisely, for each technology (Java, PHP, .NET, etc.) and each type of repository (database, LDAP directory, mainframe, etc.) a custom data-access library should be defined and its use made mandatory. These libraries should provide customized data access for the data structures specific to the company. Usage rules should be enacted as to which technology should

---

4 ETL = Extract Transform Load.

be used in which case and when exceptions to the standard rules can be tolerated. A technical expert should be appointed for each technology. The expert will be the privileged interlocutor for project teams when they need assistance or advice on that technology. Code reviews should include a rigorous check that the standards have actually been implemented. Up-to-date documentation should be maintained under the responsibility of the global team in charge of the design of the data-access libraries. This documentation should be readily available to all IT teams and training provided when necessary.

Palliative actions often come down to centralizing things that were scattered over time. Preventive actions, on the other hand, should aim to limit the allowed technologies (databases, middleware, directories, etc.).

5.3.2.2. *Changing requirements*

Data structures are notoriously difficult and expensive to change because they have a global impact on many applications and services. The data elements that are expected to need flexibility in the future should be anticipated early on. Otherwise, unexpected changes will always increase the chances for future inconsistencies.

5.3.2.2.1. Evaluation

The aim is mostly to identify accidental redundancies, inconsistencies, and ambiguities that have accumulated over time because of previous changes in requirements. These might be the future sources of uncontrolled complexity. This is really the topic of MDM. See also the evaluation in section 5.3.2.1.

5.3.2.2.2. Simplicity actions

Simplicity actions more or less all imply various forms of reuse. One important form of reuse in the context of data access is semantic and syntactic.

> Whenever a data model has been defined by an industry sector, as an XML schema or set of UML classes, it should be systematically used, either "as is" or in an extended form.

Finding out whether such a model exists may require conducting a little investigation with partners or competitors in the same industry. Such models indeed capitalize a huge amount of experience and using them will strongly mitigate the risk of extensive changes of the data structure in the future. On the other hand, when no such model exists, creating pivot formats, which ease the exchange of data between services, follows the same logic. Because of the extensive amount of work this usually implies, such a pivot format should, however, focus only on the core business activities and the essential business applications and services.

Another form of reuse is the definition of fine-grained CRUD[5] services that can be used by more coarse-grained services.

In this context, all tasks pertaining to MDM are relevant: mapping out data structures, identifying duplicated data, removing obsolete or useless data, etc. They are all aimed at making the system more flexible.

5.3.2.3. *Human factors*

Some *multidisciplinarity* is unavoidable for the developers in charge of the data-access layer. Besides their favorite programming language, they should have at least a rudimentary knowledge of databases or LDAP directories, even when APIs exist that provide a unified access to those.

---

5 CRUD = Create, Read, Update, Delete designates a fine-grained service to handle small pieces of data.

It should be acknowledged, though, that true expertise in one domain, for example, databases, cannot be converted quickly into another expertise, for example, OOP programming, as management sometimes ingenuously seems to believe.

Proletarianization can play a significant role in the data-access layer when frameworks are used. The basic knowledge and intuition, which should guide the design of an efficient and maintainable data-access layer, is progressively lost when developers blindly use frameworks as an all-in-one solution for all persistence issues.

5.3.2.3.1. Evaluation

The only evaluation that seems practical in this context is to count the number of data-access technologies that are being used. This will, in turn, determine the number of technology experts that will be needed to provide reliable assistance on each.

5.3.2.3.2. Simplicity actions

Technological choices should be the responsibility of an architecture committee and must not be left to individual developers. The project manager must be wary of individual initiatives that deviate from the chosen standard.

Appropriate hiring, coaching, and training of IT skills are essential for mitigating the risks of disempowerment.

5.3.3. *Simplicity in software – services*

5.3.3.1. *Growing technical heterogeneity*

Technical heterogeneity can be quite high in this layer because middleware technologies and protocols abound and obsolescence is particularly quick. Physical dependencies among applications and services have a strong impact on complexity because heterogeneity will imply implementing many conversion mechanisms.

5.3.3.1.1. Evaluation

The number or redundant technologies is an obvious indicator for heterogeneity. The intricacy of the physical dependencies is also important to evaluate, as this is directly related to the quantity of protocol- or format-conversion operations that are required in a highly heterogeneous environment. Service activity monitoring tools[6] could be useful for this diagnostic.

5.3.3.1.2. Simplicity actions

As for the data-access layer, a small team of architects should enact a number of technological and design choices and be invested with sufficient authority to have theses enforced on projects. The architect team should be able to arbitrate technological choices when required.

Not believing too naively the false promises of so-called magic tools, which pretend to be able to eradicate heterogeneity, is a good idea.

A palliative action, which could help mitigate complexity, without, however, decreasing heterogeneity, is to use a service orchestrator (or ESB) that will coordinate the invocation of many services while supporting all conversion tasks to cope with the diversity of protocols. Such a choice should be made with care, though. It will be justified only when a significant number of services or applications have to be coordinated, for example, more than five, as rule of thumb. For fewer applications, it is very likely that the complexity introduced by the bus will exceed the complexity introduced by using explicit conversion mechanisms.

---

6 BAM = Business Activity Monitoring software usually includes this kind of tools.

5.3.3.2. *Changing requirements*

The service layer is in first position when dealing with changing requirements. If well designed, it should be able to absorb most of the changing requirements without excessive rework or expense. Reusability and modularity are the key here. The SOA paradigm, which has emerged over the last years, is an attempt to address this flexibility demand. Appendix 3 gives a critical review of recent SOA experiences from this perspective. For the moment, we only emphasize that services should not be defined to merely comply with some sort of fashionable architecture dogma but to address actual needs for reusing existing features, for opening parts of the system to the external world, or, ambitiously, for introducing more flexibility in business processes.

Recall also that much needless complexity can be generated when the flexibility is designed into a system that never needs it! This has been analyzed in section 4.2.

5.3.3.2.1. Evaluation

Reusability and modularity should be evaluated even though there is no obvious metric for these. Both are often related to the quality of business-object and business-process modeling and to how well this information is shared across the company.

5.3.3.2.2. Simplicity actions

A global coordination entity, with appropriate power, should be created to harmonize and enforce a strict semantic for business objects and processes to prevent ambiguities and to enable reuse across projects. This is an application of *simplicity through trust*, as minimizing ambiguities really amounts to trusting that business terms have the same meaning for everybody and that their semantic was carefully defined by qualified people.

Changing requirements are best handled when reuse is promoted by defining stable, fine-grained services on which more coarse-grained services are based. These fine-grained services should be under the responsibility of the coordination entity, too.

Managing business rules and business processes in a dedicated repository is another measure that can prove useful. Using business-rule engines may help centralize essential business rules and make their modification faster and more reliable. These are really applications of *simplicity through organization*.

Setting up a systematic and consistent modeling of business rules and business processes, which are shared and accessible, is particularly important.

Use an iterative approach to capture the most complex business rules, not at once, but by presenting users with successive partial implementations of applications, to which they can react to clarify their needs.

5.3.3.3. *Human factors*

Multidisciplinarity plays a key role when designing services, because it is in the service layer that most business requirements are translated into code. People in charge of the design of the service layer should understand the problems as they are expressed by expert business users. Simultaneously, they must also be aware of the technical constraints.

Disempowerment and proletarianization can play a significant role in the service layer when frameworks and sophisticated automation tools are used. This topic is largely discussed in section 4.3.2. The basic knowledge and intuition, which should guide the design of an efficient and maintainable data-access layer, could be lost when developers use these tools blindly. Excessive regulation, with rigid software-architecture principles, can also result in the same kind of disempowerment.

A common disempowerment situation is one in which strict rules have been enacted to ensure decoupling of layers. These usually include rules that prescribe which kind of services can call other services. In some cases, these rules may result in coding a large number of pass-through services that really do nothing, except increase the number of lines of code. Some common sense is really needed to evaluate when strict compliance to a set of rules makes sense. Common sense and experience, fortunately, cannot always be formalized.

Local interest has many different forms, the most common form being developers using their own favorite technology rather than complying with the chosen enterprise standards.

5.3.3.3.1. Evaluation

Regarding multidisciplinarity, the question to ask is simply: Is there at least one individual who has both IT and business skills? Measuring disempowerment without resorting to a psychiatrist is surely not an easy matter. The best thing is probably to try to assess, one way or another, whether people understand what they are doing and whether they understand the purpose of the software productivity tools they use. Finally, regarding the global interest, ask whether there exists a respected coordination entity.

5.3.3.3.2. Simplicity actions

Regarding the need to understand both technical and business issues, there should be, for each project, one individual (at least) who is able to record or model user requirements in a way that developers can understand. His or her job is to bridge the two worlds of business users and pure IT experts.

Regarding disempowerment, hiring and training policies are again essential. Another point worth emphasizing is that the coding and design rules should really be implemented. A large catalogue of sophisticated rules is of little use if these are not applied. Experience shows that excessive formalization, with too many rules and conventions for coding and design, systematically results in such rules not being applied. Thus, rules and best practices should be kept to a strict minimum. This minimum, however, should be known to all and should be strictly enforced.

The global team in charge of defining and checking the architecture rules are often perceived as being annoying, as they tend to slow down projects. But this is nothing more than the normal price to pay for imposing general interest over local (related to individuals or to projects) interest.

5.3.4. *Simplicity in software–user interface*

5.3.4.1. *Growing technical heterogeneity*

The domain of graphical user interfaces is probably the domain that offers the largest array of technologies: PHP, Swing, GWT, applets, JSP, JSF, Adobe Flash, Adobe Flex, Adobe Air, HTML5, Silverlight, JavaScript, Ajax, etc. to name only a few.

It is also the layer where technology is in direct contact with end users. Economic issues related to this layer are numerous, simply because it is visible. This is where the hype and fashion exist; this is where demands fluctuate most rapidly. In this layer, changing requirements really create obsolescence, which in turn progressively increases heterogeneity. This is very different from the data layer, for instance, where obsolescence is mostly generated because of changing standards and by the need for increased performance.

Heterogeneity is a fact that should be accepted, because it is nearly unavoidable. It is quite unrealistic to assume that it will be possible, in the near future, to homogenize these technologies. Thus, focus should be more on decoupling to prevent interchangeable presentation technologies from impacting other layers of the software architecture.

5.3.4.1.1. Evaluation

Evaluate the number of technologies used for each type of application: web applications, mobile applications, and desktop applications. Are there any component libraries available for each?

5.3.4.1.2. Simplicity actions

A transverse organization should define and enforce standards and rules for which technologies are allowed under what circumstances and for which type of applications (or channel).

5.3.4.2. *Changing requirements*

Changing requirements are the rule rather than the exception in this domain. They may concern superficial aspects, such as color or layout, or more complex aspects such as changing the logic of navigation between a set of pages.

5.3.4.2.1. Evaluation

Evaluate the level of reuse of components or widgets. Perform code reviews to evaluate how well the presentation layer is decoupled from the services and from the data layer. This will directly impact the complexity generated by repeated changes to the user interface. To predict how much time will be necessary to perform changes, it is useful to categorize screens of applications as *easy*, *standard*, and *complex*. Each category should be assigned a maximal duration for its design and implementation, say 2 hours, half day, and a full day, respectively. This will provide rough estimates of the complexity of the presentation layer.

5.3.4.2.2. Simplicity actions

The key words for simplicity actions in this domain are *decoupling* and *reuse*.

Decoupling means that graphical user elements should be decoupled from the rest of the architecture. This will prevent changes to user-interface features from propagating to the service layer and the other way around. This principle is actually manifested in the well-known MVC[7] design pattern.

Reuse implies defining component libraries for widgets[8] and for portlets[9] to be reused and combined as a means to match at least part of the changing requirements. Widgets are meant for developers, while portlets are for users who can customize and reposition them to fit their needs. Defining a reusable layout mechanism is another simplicity action.

But reuse should certainly not be applied in a dogmatic way, as writing disposable code could sometimes be the most sensible option. If the prescribed time limits to implement a

---

7 MVC stands for Model View Controller. It is a design pattern meant to decouple the pieces of code that are responsible for the display (V), for the business logic (C), and the data (M) being displayed.
8 A widget is a simple reusable element of a graphical user interface.
9 A portlet is a pluggable frame that is managed and displayed within a web portal.

screen or a page are exceeded too often, we should consider changing either the technology or the skills used.

We have *simplicity through reduction* and *organization* at work here.

5.3.4.3. *Human factors*

At times, proletarianization can play a role during design. Implementing a user interface is indeed a very technical topic. It is therefore essential to resort to resources who have specialized skills in one technology and who have a thorough working knowledge of the appropriate design tools. Developing screens quickly and reliably does not allow for dilettantism and manual coding should be forbidden.

For obvious productivity reasons, much of the graphical user-interface design is currently generated automatically by wizards of modern IDEs. This is where the danger for disempowerment lies. This generated code cannot be trusted blindly. Its often intricate structure must be understood by developers so that they can modify it when needed. Poor understanding will quickly generate code that is hard to maintain and increase needless complexity.

Creativity definitely has its place in the presentation layer.

5.3.4.3.1. Evaluation

Evaluate the range of skills and technologies that are necessary to develop user interfaces reliably for all types of clients and channels.

5.3.4.3.2. Simplicity actions

Technological choices should be the responsibility of an architecture committee and must not be left to individual developers. Project managers should be wary of individual initiatives that deviate from the chosen standard, just for fun.

Using appropriate productivity tools is essential in the presentation layer. For each user-interface technology (PHP, JSF, Swing, Struts, Silverlight, Flash, etc.), one development environment should be chosen and imposed on all developers. These tools will quickly generate the skeleton of the code, which then has to be modified manually.

5.3.5. *Simplicity in functional architecture*

5.3.5.1. *Growing technical heterogeneity*

Technical heterogeneity is of no direct relevance for the functional architecture, as technical infrastructure is not the primary concern here. It could nevertheless play a limited role when different modeling tools are used for specifying the business processes, requirements, or use cases that comprise the functional architecture.

5.3.5.1.1. Evaluation

How many different notations and tools are used to specify the functional architecture?

5.3.5.1.2. Simplicity actions

Choose a consistent and universal notation to define the functional architecture. Choose appropriate tools. Enforce these choices.

5.3.5.2. *Changing requirements*

Changing requirements impact, by definition, on the functional architecture. Useless complexity could be generated, not on a technical level, but rather on a semantic level, because of ambiguities and needless logical dependencies that could be created over time.

5.3.5.2.1. Evaluation

How much redundancy and ambiguity are present in business terms and in business processes? How much needless logical dependence has been created due to changing requirements? Are there shared repositories of business objects, business rules, and business processes?[10] If so, are these known to all concerned stakeholders? Are they used systematically? How well are changes in application features synchronized with these models? How far can previous functional changes be traced back?

5.3.5.2.2. Simplicity actions

Define a role or a team in charge of defining a consistent set of business concepts, rules, and processes. Make sure these definitions are readily available to all relevant stakeholders and that they are used effectively on projects.

Experience shows that big-bang approaches for capturing user requirements are usually doomed to failure. Iterative procedures are usually better suited for capturing a complex and unclear set of requirements. One way to achieve this is to present users with successive partial implementations of an application to which they can react to clarify their needs.

If available, reuse existing industry-wide standard models for business objects, rules, and processes. This can require some interaction with partners or competitors in the same field but is usually well worth the effort, as it is likely to mitigate the impact of future changes.

5.3.5.3. *Human factors*

Multidisciplinarity is inherent to the definition of a functional architecture, which more often than not will

---

10 This is closely related to what can be measured with the IS Rating Tool from the Sustainable IT Architecture organization, founded by Pierre Bonnet.

involve different skills. The reliability of communication between experts of different domains is essential to avoid generating needless logical complexity in the functional architecture. Technical issues cannot be neglected altogether, as requirements can never be made totally independently of technical constraints. In a way, this situation is the mirror image of the service layer, which focused mostly on technical issues.

Proletarianization of business users will occur when automation is imposed for tasks that would otherwise benefit from the imagination and creativity of experienced users. Excessive automation through rigid BPM tools can be counterproductive and should be avoided.

Global interest versus local interest is at stake, for instance, when retro-modeling is required after some functionality has changed. Such modeling normally takes place once a project is finished and is therefore often perceived as having no immediate consequences on anything. Capitalization, although it is an investment in future knowledge, is often perceived as a burden and waste of time.

5.3.5.3.1. Evaluation

Regarding multidisciplinarity, ask whether domain specialists have a reasonable understanding of their colleagues' expertise.

Regarding disempowerment, try to evaluate the proportion of business processes for which human creativity and expertise clearly outweigh the advantages of automation.

Finally, regarding global interest related to modeling (business objects, rules, and processes) ask the following: what is the degree of synchronization between models and deployed applications, assuming such models exist?

5.3.5.3.2. Simplicity actions

To face multidisciplinarity, train specialists in each other's domain of expertise to enhance communication. Try to understand why some tools (modeling tools, reporting tools, collaborative tools), which could be useful to master complexity, are not used.

To avoid demotivation and disempowerment, identify those processes that need the most creativity and imagination or fine-grained expertise and avoid automating those in rigid BPM.

Finally, regarding the need for retro-modeling, which can be assimilated to the global interest, there are no truly magical solutions. One solution is to establish rituals, which will progressively become part of the corporate technical culture. Such rituals should be supported and sponsored by management.

Conclusion

Fools ignore complexity. Pragmatists suffer it.
Some can avoid it. Geniuses remove it.
Alan Jay Perlis – Epigrams on Programming

The last quarter of a century has witnessed different periods in information system (IS) management, based on successive strategies and hopes. The initial blind faith in technological progress was first followed by cost reduction and, not long after, by value-creation strategies. Early in this book, we pointed out that there is really no single, legitimate concept of value for an IS. There are indeed many, from which we singled out three for their relevance and independence, namely the use value, the strategic value, and the particularly important sustainability value. We argued that these three concepts really cover the interest of most IS stakeholders. Acting efficiently on these values cannot be achieved using some sort of "black-box view" of information. What is needed is a more lucid understanding of the underpinnings of value creation or destruction, especially in those areas where technical and human aspects are most entangled. IT professionals and top management should progressively work towards a more lucid, "white-box view" of ISs, rather than relying excessively on mechanical rules and blind procedures. The general idea is that, ultimately, creation of value is creation of appropriate forms of simplicity for different stakeholders.

As a first step to better define simplicity, we tried, somewhat paradoxically, to understand the easier ideas of complexity! The results of information theory, considered a provider of a robust set of metaphors of complexity, taught us a number of important lessons. Just as for the idea of value, we learned that there is no single legitimate concept of complexity. At the deepest conceptual level, complexity can be related to unpredictability of a system, to randomness of a structure, or to the logical depth, that is the amount of design, that went into the system. We learned that complexity concepts that are both computable (or measurable) and universally applicable to any system simply do not exist. Specific concepts, on the other hand, do exist and they are useful, provided they are strictly applied to their limited domain of validity. Some, like cyclomatic complexity, are well known in software engineering, while others, like the horizontal and vertical complexity, that we introduced ourselves, prove useful when it comes to relating complexity and creation of value.

The second step, toward making simplicity practical, was to define six general principles. These principles were inspired by various thoughts on the design of objects. Simplicity turns out to be much harder to define than complexity. This is because, on the one hand, there is no mathematical counterpart that could guide us, but also and more importantly, because the idea of simplicity fundamentally involves non-formalized human factors. However, this difficulty, related to human factors, is precisely also what makes it more useful than complexity. The multifaceted concept of simplicity was split into six fundamental simplicity principles: simplicity by reduction, by hiding complexity, by organization, by learning, by time saving, and finally by trust. Some of these principles bear a close resemblance to the principles of the Lean Software Management for which they provide, we believe, a deeper conceptual foundation.

After identifying and organizing the main sources of uncontrolled complexity in ISs, namely growing technical heterogeneity, changing requirements, and a selection of human factors, we described how the above-mentioned simplicity principles can be used together to limit the effect of those sources and, thereby, we identified practical means of enhancing our triplet of values. In Chapter 5, we proposed a list of simplicity best practices, organized according to the layer of the IS architecture to which they apply: hardware, software, or functional architecture.

So, what could be the single most salient message of simplicity we are trying to convey? We believe that simplicity is a set of intuitions, a culture, and a set of values that do not necessarily readily translate into algorithms, templates, or frameworks. We believe it should be acknowledged, by IT professionals and top management, that, in the end, there is really only one efficient tool to master complexity: the human mind. Now, a human mind, to function efficiently, should *not* be used (at least not only) as a machine that merely implements algorithms and uses templates. This will inevitably create demotivation and disempowerment in the long run, which only generate more uncontrollable complexity. Higher abilities, which thus far remain the monopoly of the human mind, such as making sound critical judgments, developing simplicity intuitions, and achieving global understanding, should not be overlooked if we want to have a chance of mastering complexity. For this to be possible, stakeholders, each at their own level, should have the feeling that their work makes sense.

APPENDICES

Appendix 1

Digging into Information Theory

A1.1. Shannon entropy[1]

In the late 1940s, Claude Shannon was working on encoding problems at Bell Labs. More specifically, Shannon was interested in establishing reliable transmission of information between a sender S and a recipient R. Think of S as randomly generating messages composed of sequences of words. The fundamental question Shannon was trying to solve is: what is the optimal encoding that makes the encoded messages as short as possible and what is the average length of these encoded words?

The intuition behind the solution that he found is easy to grasp:

> Frequent words should be encoded with short strings, whereas infrequent words can be encoded with longer strings.

---

1 Our presentation is inspired by the excellent book by J.-L. Delahaye [DEL 99], to which we refer the interested reader for more details.

In this section, we will show how the randomness of messages that S generates is actually related to the amount of information contained in those messages.

Remember that the three forms of information theory complexity that we review in this appendix are all defined as the value of information contained in binary strings once a goal has been specified for what to do with these strings. For the case at hand, Shannon entropy, the goal is to compress the random messages that S sends, as much as possible.

Let us be just a little bit more precise here. Assume that the sender S uses only a finite number N of words that we denote w_i where the index i runs from 1 to N. Assume, moreover, that the words w_i are generated with probabilities p_i (numbers that sum up to 1). Let us then denote by $l\ (w_i)$ the length of the encoded version of w_i. The average length of encoded words sent by S is simply $\sum_i p_i\ l(p_i)$. This is precisely the quantity that an optimal encoding should make as small as possible. Shannon was able to find such an optimal coding[2] (based on some mild technical assumptions about encodings). He also found an explicit formula (that we prove here) for the optimal length, which is $l(w_i) = \log(1/p_i)$. As expected, small p_is lead to large lengths.

Plugging in these optimal lengths in the average length, we get $\sum_i p_i\ \log(1/p_i)$ for the average length of the optimally encoded words. Shannon called this quantity the entropy of the source S and denoted it with H. Let us emphasize that this quantity H depends only on the probabilities p_i and not on the words w_i themselves. Following Shannon, we now argue that H is really a measure of the amount of disorder in the set of words produced by S.

---

2 The optimal coding is known as the *Shannon-Fano* code (see [GRU 04]).

Before continuing, note that the quantity $H = \sum_i p_i \log(1/p_i)$ can be defined as soon as probabilities p_i of some events are available, independently of the existence of words w_i. The entropy concept thus has broader significance than just for coding issues. The coding interpretation is useful, however, because it clarifies the relation of H with other concepts such as information, which is our main concern in this book. A convincing connection of H with complexity will have to await the next section on K-complexity.

To get a better intuition of why H is indeed a measure of randomness, let us look at the possible outcomes of throwing a six-sided dice, thus $N = 6$ here. If the dice is fair, each side has the same probability $p_i = 1/6$ of appearing. The entropy H of such a situation is readily computed, it equals $\log 6 \approx 2.58$. If, on the other hand, the dice had only 6s on each face we could be sure that a 6 comes out in any case. In this new situation, $p_6 = 1$, whereas $p_1 = \ldots = p_5 = 0$. In this case, H is zero[3]. The former situation has a higher value of randomness $H = 2.58$ than the latter, which has $H = 0$, just as we expect.

These simple observations actually generalize in a straightforward way. It can easily be proven that the maximal entropy is always reached when p_i are all equal to $1/N$; recall that N is the number of possible outcomes. These are the situations where we have strictly no clue about the outcomes of the probabilistic events. Entropy H in such cases is just $\log N$. By contrast, in a situation where we know the outcome for sure, H is always zero.

There is a useful rephrasing of the above, that relates the concepts of entropy H and information, which is perhaps more familiar. In a situation where $H = 0$, in other words, when there is no unpredictability at all, we really learn nothing. We already knew the result in advance! By

---

3 Because $0 \log 0$ really equals 0 when things are carefully worked out.

contrast, when H is maximal, we have no prior knowledge of the outcome and thus we really gain information when we discover which event (or word) occurred. The information gained from a random source is thus greater the higher the unpredictability or randomness of that source is.

The Shannon entropy H is a convenient and universal measure of this unpredictability of a random source. The interpretation of H as an average encoding length also shows that encoding highly random messages, or equivalent messages that convey much information, requires code words that on average are longer than for non-random source.

> It is more costly to encode information from a very unpredictable source than from a predictable one.

Innumerable uses have been made of the Shannon entropy in all areas of engineering and applied sciences, from biology to object-oriented programming. Too often, however, the need for a genuine probabilistic setting, beyond which H has no clear interpretation, has been overlooked.

A1.2. Shannon entropy in short

For further reference, let us summarize the most important properties of Shannon entropy:

– It measures the *amount of randomness* present in a system. This can be interpreted as some peculiar form of complexity as we shall justify more explicitly in the next section.

– The concept of entropy arises naturally when optimizing the encoding of random messages. The goal mentioned in the introduction is to *compress as much as possible a random message* for which the probabilities of words are known. The randomness of these messages (or complexity, or information) is high if their optimal compression is on average long.

– Shannon entropy is *easy to compute*, provided the probabilities p_i exist and are known.

We emphasize once more that we will not make any explicit use of the entropy formula H within IT but shall use these reflections as our first input for what complexity can mean in a context where randomness is present in a system. As we shall see shortly, it also provides a natural introduction for our next concept.

A1.3. Kolmogorov complexity

One of the most obvious shortcomings of the Shannon entropy H is that it only allows assigning a measure of randomness or complexity to messages S comprised *random* words w_i. What, however, if we are interested in the complexity of just one single word w_i or of a single object? It turns out that another concept of complexity can be used for this purpose. This is precisely what Kolmogorov complexity achieves and we now briefly introduce it on a heuristic level.

The idea that Kolmogorov proposed in the 1960s is again related to a concept of optimal compression. This time, however, we look at a single binary string or message s and ask: "What is the optimal compression of that single string?" We suppose we have some generic computing mechanism at hand, something like an abstract computer. Let us denote it by T and assume it can be programmed in the usual sense. Let us denote by p a program, thought of as a binary string, in any language understood by T. When p runs on T, it produces a result s that is itself a binary string. We write that $s = T(p)$. What is the optimal compression for a single string s? For a given computer T, the optimal compression of a string s might be defined as the shortest program p_{min} that, when run on T, gives s as a result. In other words, $s = T(p_{min})$. The Kolmogorov complexity $K(s)$ of this string s is then simply defined as the length of this optimal program p_{min}.

Thus, $K(s) = \text{length}(p_{min})$.

> The K-complexity $K(s)$ of a string s is the length of the shortest program p_{min} that produces it.

This new concept of complexity fits quite well in the general context where the measure of complexity is the value of information with respect to some goal. The goal here is simply: "compress the single string as much as possible".

Let us illustrate this definition with three simple examples (assume they have comparable length, say one billion bytes):

$s_{\text{alternating}}$ = 10101010101010101010...

$s_{\text{prime numbers}}$ = 02030507011013017019...

$s_{\text{random stuff}}$ = 10948566028350295456...

The sequence $s_{\text{alternating}}$ is extremely simple in the sense that a very short program will be able to produce it. The next sequence, $s_{\text{prime numbers}}$, which lists prime numbers separated by a zero will need a slightly longer program. The last sequence $s_{\text{random stuff}}$ is completely random. The only program that produces it is an explicit print operation for that particular string. The size of this program will be slightly above the length of the string: in this case, one billion. We can thus classify the above sequences according to their Kolmogorov complexity:

$$K(s_{\text{alternating}}) < K(s_{\text{prime numbers}}) < K(s_{\text{random stuff}}) \approx 10^9$$

As it stands, this definition would seem to entail a great deal of arbitrariness. Indeed it looks like $K(s)$ is strongly dependent on both the machine T and the programming language we use for writing our shortest program p_{min}. Information theory teaches us, however, that this is not true. It was Turing's discovery in the 1930s that stated that there exists a universal computing mechanism. They are traditionally referred to as Turing machines and are, conceptually, just as powerful as any modern computer (they can perform the same tasks), hence the adjective "universal". Our T is such a Turing machine. What makes K-complexity really meaningful is that it can be proved that $K(s)$ does not depend very strongly[4] on which Turing machine we choose in the definition. This might perhaps sound amazing or unintuitive, but it is nevertheless true and is the real foundation of algorithmic complexity theory.

On a metaphoric level, we can summarize the above as follows:

An object or a sequence s is K-complex if its shortest possible description is long.

---

4 What can be proved is that two different Turing machines T_1 and T_2 lead two concepts of complexity $K_1(s)$ and $K_2(s)$, which differ only by a constant, independent of s, that is obviously of no importance provided we are interested in long sequences s. Kolmogorov complexity is therefore only an asymptotic concept.

A1.4. Choosing a scale of description

When examining the complexity of an object, an information system (IS), a molecule, or a living being, we claimed above that it is enough to look at its binary description s. However, for such a description to really make sense, we should first choose an appropriate scale of description for the object under consideration. Taking an example from IT, the description of an IS at the level of computer chips is certainly not the same as describing the same IS at the level of the source code of the software, which is still different from describing the set of business objects and business processes. A fine-grained description s_{fine} contains typically much more information than a coarse-grained description s_{coarse}. The point here is that more information does not necessarily mean more useful information. A description s_{fine} could be useless because the information of interest to us is hidden in huge amount of mostly irrelevant information. Conversely, a description s_{coarse} could be useless because it is just too coarse!

These remarks point out the necessity to choose an appropriate level of abstraction when describing objects or systems that involve different scales. ISs are definitely in this category. Choosing a level of abstraction implies, among other things, describing an object with just the information of interest for a particular purpose, forgetting smaller scale details. This is a delicate issue when modeling ISs, with UML diagrams for instance. This topic is discussed more in depth in section 2.3.2.

K-complexity is an intrinsic attribute of a binary string. It is not, however, an intrinsic attribute of an object in the physical world, which requires choosing a scale for its description.

Thus, even though the K-complexity manages to remove the arbitrariness in the evaluation of complexity related to choosing a description mechanism (the T mentioned above), it does *not* remove the arbitrariness related to choosing an appropriate scale of description of an object.

A1.5. Relation to Shannon entropy

There is a simple relation between the Shannon entropy and the K-complexity that helps justify our previous claim that Shannon entropy is related to an idea of complexity, which is really our main concern.

Recall that the Shannon entropy H can only be defined when probabilities p_i are defined on a set of words or elementary messages w_i, whereas K-complexity measures complexity for each single w_i separately. It is thus hard to resist the temptation to ask: "What is the average of the individual K-complexities $K(w_i)$ of those words w_i when the probabilities p_i are used as weights?" The answer is quite simple (provided the p_i is not too "complicated" in a precise sense): it is just the Shannon entropy H! In other words, the Shannon entropy is nothing but an average version of the K-complexity. The two concepts are thus compatible and complementary.

A1.6. Computing the Kolmogorov complexity

Now, assume we have an object for which we chose an appropriate description level and whose K-complexity we would like to compute. Is there any method or algorithm to compute K or, at least, an approximation thereof? Well, perspectives look rather grim here unfortunately. As a matter of fact, information theory tells us that, except for exceptionally simple binary sequences s, the complexity $K(s)$

cannot be computed by any algorithmic means.[5] In other words, there is no efficient way to compute the number $K(s)$, efficient meaning here: computable in a predictable length of time. It is essential to understand that this is not due to some lack of skill or lack of imagination of mathematicians or engineers, but that this is an intrinsic property of questions related to finding optimal programs such as p_{min}. The lesson is that computing complexity is most often so hard that it is practically infeasible.

Facing such a reality, we might relax our requirements and ask whether we can at least find some decent approximation of $K(s)$. The good news is: yes, it is indeed possible to find computable approximations of $K(s)$. The bad news, however, is that it is impossible to know the quality of such approximations, making them of little practical use.

This might seem somewhat depressing, but we cannot just ignore these facts. We draw the following conclusions:

– Even a concept of complexity defined using such a simple goal as mentioned above (compress s as much as possible) is extremely hard to compute. Unsurprisingly, things can only get worse when the goal becomes more realistic. The previous G related to evaluating a compiled code was such an example. Complexity is really an intrinsically difficult topic. Thus, any claim for an easy solution for computing or optimizing it is necessarily wrong.

– Even if the optimal or shortest description (p_{min} mentioned above) of an object (s mentioned above) is impossible to discover in a reasonable time, comparing two descriptions to find the shortest could be achievable and useful.

– One possible way out of the non-computability trap could be to abandon the quest for a universal concept of

---

5 For the mathematically inclined reader, this can be traced back to limitations implied by Gödel's theorem.

complexity altogether. As we just realized, such concepts are of low practical interest, except for supplying some healthy intuition. The contrapositive formulation is that useful or computable versions of complexity can only have limited meaning for some very specific types of objects or structures. Such examples were given in section 2.3.1.

A1.7. Kolmogorov complexity in short

Let us summarize what we have learned so far regarding K-complexity:

– K-complexity is a concept that *applies to single binary strings describing any kind of object or system. $K(s)$ is really an intrinsic property of s*.

– In contrast with the Shannon entropy H, the K-complexity $K(s)$ is *most often impossible to evaluate and even to approximate* efficiently. This difficulty is intrinsic to the problem at hand. No future improvement in engineering science will ever improve this situation.

– Describing an object or a system with a binary string *entails choosing a scale* of description, or an abstraction level, that keeps only relevant information. This arbitrariness is impossible to remove and must be taken seriously.

– The *Shannon entropy can be seen as an averaged version of K-complexity*.

Besides the already mentioned practical limitations to the K-complexity, there is another, more conceptual, problem we now briefly address.

A1.8. Bennett's logical depth

Let us briefly come back to the example mentioned above and look once more at $s_{\text{prime numbers}}$ and $s_{\text{random stuff}}$. Both sequences are complex and have higher K-complexity than $s_{alternating}$. However, they are complex in very different ways: $s_{prime\ numbers}$ is complex because it needs some amount of calculation to be performed, namely computing a long sequence of prime numbers. By contrast, $s_{random\ stuff}$ is complex because there is no way to compress it. It is just irreducibly complicated.

Thus, we see that K-complexity can assign high complexity to random objects and low complexity to organized objects. Keeping ISs in mind, we now realize that, after all, K-complexity is perhaps not such a good measure of the kind of complexity we are interested in. We would like to distinguish *complicated systems*, which are systems that have no short description, from *complex systems*, which require a lot of effort to produce. The table below summarizes the main differences we expect between these two forms of complexity.

Complicated objects	Organized objects
Their description is long.	Their description could be either long or short.
Random objects are always complicated.	Random objects are not organized objects.
They are easy to produce.	They require design or computing to be produced.
They can be produced very quickly; they even occur spontaneously.	They grow slowly; they never occur spontaneously.

Is there a mathematical formalization for this kind of organized complexity? Indeed there is. It is called Bennett's logical depth – named after its inventor. The associated theory is, however, less developed than for K-complexity.

Bennett's logical depth formalizes the idea that what determines the value of a system or some information is the cost of the computing effort needed to produce it. A goal appropriate for the question at hand would be something like: "find a description of s that requires as little computation as possible to produce s".

The first attempt to define organized complexity is to simply mimic the definition of K-complexity. That is, replace, in that definition, the shortest program p_{min} with the fastest program p_{fast}. Unfortunately, it turns out that this does not work for two reasons. First, it is not very hard to prove that this definition leads to a measure of complexity, which is simply proportional to the length of the binary string s (whose complexity we are trying to evaluate). This obviously is not very exciting. Second, no universality can be proved. In contrast with K-complexity, this definition does depend strongly on which Turing machine T we select.

An appropriate definition was proposed in the late 1970s by Charles H. Bennett. It is called the Bennett logical depth $D(s)$ and is defined as the number of steps necessary for the minimal program p_{min} running on a Turing machine (the same as in K-complexity!) to produce s. The good news is that this definition can be proved to be very robust. First, $D(s)$, like $K(s)$ before, does not depend on T too much, making it an intrinsic property of s. Second, programs p, which are not strictly minimal, but only close to p_{min}, are acceptable as well. To summarize:

> An object has large Bennett logical depth if it encapsulates a great amount of computation.

There is bad news too, unfortunately, which is quite similar to that for K-complexity. That is, $D(s)$ is most often impossible to calculate practically and even to approximate efficiently.

When attempting to describe the depth D for an object or a system, rather than for a binary strings s, we must choose a scale of description, just as for K-complexity.

To gain some intuition, let us look at some simple examples from the IT world, using the above-mentioned concepts as metaphors.

	Low K-complexity (short description)	High K-complexity (long description)
Low Bennett depth (low design effort)	Standard piece of code that is generated automatically. Code for CRUD[6] operations belong here for instance	Databases with lots of unstructured information.
High Bennett depth (high design effort)	Simple business rules that need to be coded by hand because they are non-standard.	Large and well structured databases. Large and well structured code.

ISs taken as a whole are obviously both deep and K-complex. Practical complexity metrics for ISs will only apply to some layers and to some limited aspects of enterprise architecture (see Appendix 2).

A1.9. Bennett's logical depth in short

Let us summarize what we have learned about Bennett's logical depth:

– Bennett's logical depth is a robust *formalization of organizational complexity* in the sense that it measures the

---

6 CRUD is an acronym for Create, Read, Update and Delete which are the basic data-manipulation operations on any set of data.

amount of computing required to construct an object starting from its optimally compressed description.

– It corresponds to a goal, which is: "Find a description that requires as little computation as possible to produce the object".

– Just as K-complexity it is *hard to compute* in practice and hard even to approximate efficiently.

Appendix 2

Two Measures of Code Complexity

A2.1. Cyclomatic complexity

Among the myriad of metrics of code complexity available, cyclomatic complexity is probably the best known. Most code analysis tools can measure it.

> Cyclomatic complexity aims to measure the amount of decision logic encapsulated in a software module or a function.

For simplicity, we shall assume henceforth that there is a single point of entry and a single exit point to the module whose complexity we wish to evaluate. Cyclomatic complexity is defined by first associating a control-flow graph to the code under consideration. Nodes in this graph represent elementary statements, while edges, which have a direction, represent transfer of control between these statements. This control-flow graph represents all possible execution paths through the module.

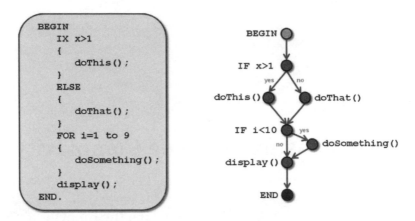

Figure A2.1. *The flow graph associated to a piece of code containing one decision and one loop*

The earlier definition of Shannon entropy could perhaps encourage us to define the complexity of the code simply as the total number of such execution paths (or its logarithm). This, however, would not account for the over-counting due to the many paths that are not truly independent. In other words, we should be aware that many paths can be obtained by combination of others. Cyclomatic complexity C_{cycl} precisely takes this into account and, assuming an entry point and an exit point are defined, it is defined by[1]:

> C_{cycl} is the minimum number of independent paths through the control-flow graph that can generate all possible paths by mere combination.

This rather abstract-looking definition of C_{cycl} fortunately turns out to be very easy to compute. Let E and N denote,

---

1 A rigorous definition of the concept of path independence would be outside the scope of this book. The mathematically inclined reader might want to review the concept of the first homology group of a graph. Cyclomatic complexity is actually nothing but the cardinality of this group.

respectively, the number of edges and the number of nodes in the control-flow graph. Then

$$C_{cycl} = E - N + 2.$$

The formula is so simple that many books take it as the definition. But this really obscures the true combinatorial significance of the cyclomatic complexity in terms of independent paths. Further insight into this quantity is gained by considering two more facts. Let $N_{test\ cases}$ denote the number of tests cases necessary to cover all execution branches of the module and $N_{if\ statements}$ be the number of "IF" statements in the module. Naturally, we could expect the number of test cases to coincide with the number of independent paths. However, the logic of the program might forbid some combinations, thus

$$C_{cycl} \geq N_{test\ cases}.$$

In other words, the number of test cases is never larger than the cyclomatic complexity. Thus, C_{cycl} can be seen as a measure of the amount of effort to test the program. There is another statement, which substantiates the idea that C_{cycl} measures something like an amount of logical complexity contained in a software module and, hence, the amount of effort to produce to understand it, namely

$$C_{cycl} = N_{if\ statements} + 1.$$

This second statement is less obvious, but it is nevertheless true.

Practical wisdom has suggested that a module should not have a cyclomatic complexity much larger than 10. There is substantial evidence that beyond that limit the code becomes just too complicated to be maintained reliably.

Thus, C_{cycl} has some very loose relation to something like Shannon entropy, provided we are ready to accept that the various paths are followed randomly (which, strictly speaking, is of course wrong). It is also loosely related to the "Learn" facet of simplicity as we just noticed. On a more fundamental and quantitative level, however, there is no relation with the concepts from information theory.

Finally, let us mention that the etymology of "cyclomatic" is related to the fact that the C_{cycl}, when defined by $E - N + 1$, is the number of cycles in an undirected graph.

A2.2. An example of a scale-invariant complexity measure

Intuitively, scale-invariance for a metric of complexity refers to the idea that complexity should remain independent of the scale of description. To define a scale-invariant measure more formally, the first step is to define a mathematically practical abstraction of a multiscale architecture. *Recursive graphs* do just this[2]. Rather than giving a formal definition, we simply describe it using Figure A2.2:

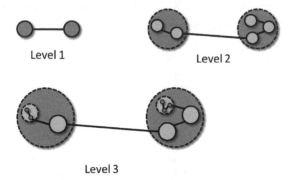

Figure A2.2. *An example of recursive graph with three levels*

---

2 We follow here the treatment proposed in Yves Caseau [CAS 07].

A recursive graph G is nothing but a finite sequence of graphs $G = (G_1, ..., G_n)$, where G_1 is the graph with coarsest scale (with least details). G_n is the graph with smallest scale (with most details), in fact it is the one that contains all information about a multiscale structure. A graph G_k is made up of a collection V_k of vertices connected by a set L_k of links. The graph G_{k-1} describes a coarser view of G_k in the sense that it contains less information. More precisely, a node in V_{k-1} is a non-empty collection of vertices from V_k and a link in L_{k-1} is also a link in L_k (but not necessarily the other way around). Going from G_1 to G_2 until G_n is like zooming-in across a multiscale structure, each step revealing further details.

With these definitions in mind, we can now formulate more precisely what we mean by scale-invariance. To do this, we define two operations on recursive graphs, a zoom-out operation Z and a zoom-in operation X. The first is defined in the following way:

$$Z[(G_1, ..., G_{n-1}, G_n)] = (G_1, ..., G_{n-1}).$$

Note that the Z zoom-out mapping just erases the information contained in the finest grained graph G_n of the multigraph G. It is really a view of the same system at a larger scale. It is thus a non-invertible mapping and, strictly speaking, a zoom-in operation cannot be defined. A partial inverse can, however, be defined in the following way. First, consider all recursive graphs G such that $Z[G] = (G_1, ..., G_{n-1})$. Second, from this (actually infinite) set keep only those graphs $(G_1, ..., G_{n-1}, G_n)$ which satisfy the following two conditions:

– Given a node v in V_{n-1}, the set of vertices in G_n that map to this v under Z should form a complete graph.

– If vertices u_1 and u_2 in G_n map under Z to two vertices v_1 and v_2 in V_{n-1}, which are connected by a link in L_{n-1}, then u_1 and u_2 should be connected by a link in L_n. Thus, the finer-scale nodes are supposed to be maximally connected. This is surely a strong restriction on the structure of graphs, but it is indeed necessary to make things work.

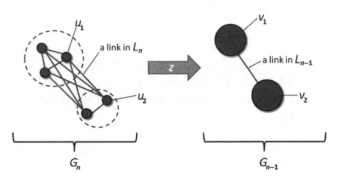

Figure A2.3. *The nodes in G_n should be maximally connected*

Let us then denote $X[(G_1, \dots, G_{n-1})]$, this restricted set of recursive graphs. Now, obviously, for any $H = ((G_1, \dots, G_{n-1}, H_n))$ belonging to the set $X[(G_1, \dots, G_{n-1})]$ we have, by definition of the mapping X, $Z[H] = (G_1, \dots, G_{n-1})$. Thus, X is a sort of inverse mapping for the zoom-out mapping Z.

One simple and useful extension of recursive graphs, that we shall need, is that of weighted recursive graphs. It allows us to take into account a unit cost associated to each node of the recursive graph. We assume that there is one weight function w_i for each scale $i = 1, \dots, n$, which associates a number $w_i(v)$ to each node v in V_i.

One crucial assumption regarding the set of weight functions w_i is their additivity.

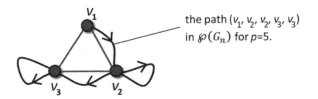

the path $(v_1, v_2, v_2, v_3, v_3)$
in $\wp(G_n)$ for $p=5$.

Figure A2.4. *An example of a path in $\wp(G_n)$ with repetitions at vertices v_2 and v_3*

More specifically, the weight $w_i(v)$ of a node v in V_i is supposed to be the sum of the weights $w_{i+1}(u)$ of the vertices u in V_{i+1} that have been identified in v, explicitly:

$$w_i(v) = \sum_{u \in v} w_{i+1}(u).$$

This is an assumption that puts strong limits on the semantics of the weight system $(w_i)_{1...n}$. In particular, this assumption prevents taking into account more complicated aggregations of complexity that would not follow from mere addition of weights. The true reason for this restriction on the weights $(w_i)_{i=1...n}$ is simply that it allows us to define a scale-invariant complexity measure. Other, more general weight functions, would not allow this. It is thus important to check that a system of weight functions taken from real IT life satisfies, at least approximately, this assumption.

Scale-invariant measures of complexity $C^{(p)}$, where p is an arbitrary integer, are then defined. For a recursive graph $G = (G_1, ..., G_n)$, endowed with a weight system $w = (w_i)_{i=1...n}$, the complexity is then defined as follows

$$C^{(p)}[G, w] = \left(\sum_{(v_1,...,v_p) \in \wp(G_n)} w_n(v_1) ... w_n(v_p) \right)^{1/p}.$$

The sum here is over all paths $(v_1, \ldots, v_p)$ in the set $\wp(G_n)$ of paths *with* repetitions in the finest scale graph G_n in the recursive graph G. That repetitions are allowed means that a path can connect a node with itself.

The complexity $C^{(p)}[G]$ has the following remarkable properties:

1) $C^{(p)}[G]$ is *linear in the weight w* in the sense that $C^{(p)}[G, \lambda w] = \lambda\, C^{(p)}[G, w]$. This property is trivial, since the pth root compensates for the factor λ^p from the p factors w_n inside the sum. In other words:

> Multiplying all the weights by some factor simply multiplies the complexity by the same factor.

2) $C^{(p)}[G]$ *is scale-invariant* under *zoom-out transformations* in the sense that $C^{(p)}[Z[G], w] = C^{(p)}[G, w]$.

> The complexity of a recursive graph G and that of its zoomed-out version $Z[G]$ are the same.

This follows immediately by first substituting $w_{n-1}(v) = \sum_{u \in v} w_n(u)$ in the sum defining $C^{(p)}[Z[G], w]$ and then by grouping paths at level n according to paths at level $n - 1$.

3) $C^{(p)}[G]$ *is scale-invariant under zoom-in transformations* as described by the zoom-in operation X defined earlier. Recall that for any H in $X[(G_1, \ldots, G_{n-1})]$, we have $Z[H] = (G_1, \ldots, G_{n-1})$. For such an H, we have $C^{(p)}[H, w'] = C^{(p)}[G, w]$, provided the original weight system w is extended to a weight system w' that now includes weights w'_n on the smaller scale G_n. In order for scale-invariance to hold, the weights w_{n-1} on each node $u \in V_{n-1}$ should be distributed

evenly across all $v \in u$ where, remember, $v \in V_n$. More explicitly, if $|u|$ is the number of V_n vertices inside u, then $w'_n(v) \equiv w_{n-1}(u)/|u|$ for any $v \in u$.

The complexity of a recursive graph G and that of any of its zoomed-in versions in $X[G]$ are the same, provided the weights are distributed evenly on the smallest scale.

This again follows from simple combinatorial analysis.

Properties 2 and 3 really justify the wording *scale-invariant complexity* for the metric $C^{(p)}[G, w]$ of a weighted, recursive graph. The case $p = 1$ is really trivial as it does not take into account the structure of the graph. The first non-trivial case is actually $p = 2$ and this is therefore the most common value chosen for p as it is also quite easy to compute in practice.

Examples

To gain some intuition for this complexity measure, let us look at the following two examples.

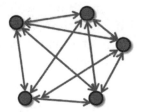 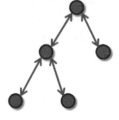

Figure A2.5. *The spaghetti graph and the hierarchical graph*

First, let us look at the spaghetti architecture $G_{\text{spaghetti}}$ with n nodes. Set any p and give equal weights $w_i = 1$ to all nodes. Since the spaghetti graph is nothing but the complete graph and since we must sum over paths *with* repeated vertices, each node v in the path $(v_1, \ldots, v_p)$ can be chosen independently. There are n^p of them, from which we conclude that

$$C^{(p)}\left[G_{\text{spaghetti}}, w\right] = (n^p \cdot 1)^{1/p} = n.$$

Second, let us look at a hierarchical architecture $G_{\text{hierachical}}$ with n nodes. Once a starting node v_1 has been chosen, each node v in the path $(v_1, \ldots, v_p)$ can be chosen in at most four different ways, thus this time we have

$$C^{(p)}\left[G_{\text{hierachical}}, w\right] \leq (n \cdot 4^p \cdot 1)^{1/p} = 4n^{1/p}.$$

Provided that n is large enough and $p \geq 2$, we see that $C^{(p)}\left[G_{\text{spaghetti}}, w\right] \gg C^{(p)}\left[G_{\text{hierachical}}, w\right]$, which accounts for the intuitive fact that spaghetti architectures are messier than hierarchical architectures!

A2.3. Conclusion

In this section, we investigate the possibility of defining a scale-invariant measure of complexity. It is indeed possible to define such a quantity, even though this imposes some rather drastic limitations. First, on how weights for individual nodes should be related at different scales. Then, on how the descriptions of the system at various scales are related when going from large to small scales.

> For the special case $p = 2$ this scale-invariant complexity measure is quite easy to compute in practice.

This measure of complexity has no relation with the deep concepts from information theory discussed in section 2.1.1. The metric $C^{(p)}$ combines two ingredients to provide a measure of complexity, namely the weights on the nodes (through the factors $w_n(v_j)$) of the multigraph and the combinatorial analysis of the links between those nodes (through the sum over paths in $\wp(G_n)$). The price to pay for computability, as we announced, is some arbitrariness and even some artificialness in the definition.

Let us emphasize that *the requirement of scale-invariance that led us to define $C^{(p)}$ is in no way essential*. Neither is the additivity of weights a natural condition. We believe this is a good illustration of the *high level of arbitrariness implied by computable complexity measures*. In this book, we shall instead consider the various scales present in an information system architecture as being independent. Complexity or simplicity should be analyzed within each scale. Nothing is assumed in general about the possibility of adding or combining complexities associated with different scales.

Appendix 3

Why Has SOA Failed So Often?

A.3.1. The need for flexibility

Facing competition that becomes tougher day after day, many large companies have struggled to improve the flexibility of their business processes and thereby gain an advantage over their competitors. Aligning the information system to business processes in order to decrease the "time to market" became the new motto. Service-oriented architecture (SOA) has been one of the most advocated solutions to meet this flexibility requirement. As a matter of fact, the various service-oriented approaches have attempted to solve two separate problems: the first is that of *reusing* existing components and the second is the *flexibility* of business processes. In section 4.2, we presented various forms of reuse as solutions to the flexibility of requirements but obviously there are situations in which reuse is justified independently of any need for flexibility. Applying *simplicity through reduction* or *simplicity through organization* could indeed be legitimate enough reasons for reuse. Opening the system to the external world can also be considered a specific form of legitimate reuse.

As was discussed in section 5.2, three layers are traditionally considered in software architecture: the data access layer, the service layer, and the user-interface layer.

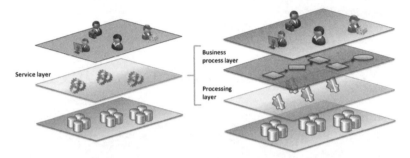

Figure A3.1. *SOA amounts to splitting the service layer into a business-process and a processing layer*

Roughly speaking, introducing SOA into a classical three-tier architecture amounts to splitting the service layer into two sub-layers: a *business-process* layer and a *processing layer*. The processing layer is responsible for implementing various business rules. It thus brings, essentially, reuse. The business-process layer, on the other hand, brings flexibility by allowing, at least in principle, recombination of services from the processing layer in different ways.

In fact, this approach has only rarely kept its promises, at least as far as flexibility is concerned. Quite on the contrary, it has often increased complexity so much as to freeze the system in a state where no further change was possible. We provide below our interpretation of this failure.

A.3.2. First issue: no suitable enterprise architecture

There are three different types of processes in a company:

– The *business processes* such as taking orders from a customer, shipping an order, delivering a product, subscribing to a loan, and booking a trip.

– The *management processes* concern making decisions and coordinating actions within a company.

– The *support processes* such as recruitment and payroll. These are unrelated to the core business and are common to many companies.

When we speak about flexibility, this only concerns the first category mentioned above, namely the business processes on which we will now focus. Among these, many require no flexibility. Placing an order for a product that needs no specific configuration is an example. These static processes are those that largely define the enterprise architecture (which we will define shortly). Flexible processes, on the other hand, could benefit from a service approach, which allows rearranging elementary business services. Taking out a loan with an insurance company or booking a trip using several partners of a travel company are examples in this category.

Unfortunately, many companies have strived for flexibility too early, before creating a robust foundation for the well-established and stable processes. The immaturity of existing architectures has caused IT teams to invest much of their time and energy in maintaining an infrastructure for perfectly stable processes. This, in turn, has prevented any serious and reliable implementation of flexibility. This situation was diagnosed in the famous paper "Avoiding the alignment trap in IT" that we mentioned earlier in section 3.3.3.

A.3.3. Second issue: no data integration

Among companies that have attempted to implement an SOA approach, many faced the data-integration problem. By data-integration issue, we mean the necessity to define a consistent and companywide semantic and syntax for a significant set of business terms. Terms such as "customer", "subscription", and "product" must necessarily be harmonized before they can be used by services, which are shared among different business units. In large companies, as no single individual alone can master the full range of concepts and terms, a phase of modeling is necessary. The point here is that these modeling tasks can be extremely complex and heavy. They have been largely underestimated most of the time, which has thus prevented a full-scale implementation of the SOA approach.

As a matter of fact, the magnitude of the task, which requires defining a consistent business-object model for a large domain of activity (banking, insurance, telecom, distribution sector, or other industry sectors), is so important that it is out of reach for even the largest IT departments. This is more an R&D task that has to be undertaken by an industry sector as a whole[1]. This approach is, in fact, nothing but a higher order of reuse that still has to gain wider acceptance if SOA approaches are to become more than consulting pipedreams.

A.3.4. Identifying the operating model

What is traditionally called the *enterprise architecture* has two facts: one is the logical organization of business processes and the other is the IT architecture supporting these processes. Starting from the above critique, regarding flexibility, we realize that the first aim is to build a robust and perennial enterprise architecture. For this to be possible, we should identity one invariant that characterizes the way a company does business in the long run. We shall

---

1 The telecom industry has been pioneering this approach with its *TM Forum' Information Framework* (SID) (see http://www.tmforum.org/ InformationFramework/1684/home.html).

follow the work of Weil *et al.* here (see [ROS 06]) and introduce the concept of an *operating model*. One obvious first guess for such an invariant could be the business strategy of the company. The business strategy covers things like the choice of a growth mode, the relevance of investing in specific markets, or developing a particular product. The authors argue that the business strategy is definitely not an invariant, as it is likely to change with new market opportunities or constraints.

A number of studies from MIT have suggested that the appropriate invariant is instead the *operating model*, which is defined as follows.

Definition: An *operating model* for a company is the optimal choice, for producing goods and services, of two parameters:

1) The appropriate *degree of standardization* of business processes across the various organizational units of a company.

2) The appropriate level of *data integration* on which these processes are based.

Let us, in turn, define these two concepts a little more precisely.

A.3.4.1. *Data integration*

This refers to defining a consistent set of business terms and appropriate technical formats (Java interfaces, XML schemas, etc.). The integration can be performed either within a process (intra-process integration) or across processes (inter-process integration).

The question to ask to evaluate the optimal level of data integration is:

> How much does a business transaction in one business unit depend on the availability, timeliness and accuracy of data in other business units?

A *high level of data integration* will facilitate the exchange of information between applications and services as no complicated conversion will be required. Within a process, changing the scheduling of services can be considered. If data integration is inter-process, a service from one process can be added to another process. Flexibility, intelligibility, and transactional integrity are all promoted by a high level of data integration.

A *low level of data integration* has other advantages. As we have already mentioned, achieving data integration on a large, inter-process scale is a very demanding and expensive endeavor. Therefore, the most obvious advantage of a low level of data integration is simply the savings gained by not engaging in a long and risky integration process. A second advantage is that of the relative autonomy of each business unit regarding the definition of its data, something that can favor taking initiatives more easily.

A.3.4.2. *Process standardization*

Standardizing processes implies that each organizational unit will execute processes the same way.

The question to ask to evaluate the optimal level of process standardization is:

What is the benefit for the company of having all its business processes executed the same way in each of its organizational units?

A *high level of process standardization* fosters a lower variability in the execution time of processes. The overall predictability is thus improved.

A *low level of process standardization*, on the other hand, avoids the local rigidity that standardization implies. It also avoids the situation where some processes, which are locally perfectly efficient, are thrown away and replaced with global ones. Local creativity and initiative is favored.

A.3.5. Which models are compatible with SOA?

It is important to realize that neither low nor high levels of process standardization or data integration are intrinsically good or suitable by themselves. Rather, each company should identify which operating model best fits its own way of doing business. Weill and Ross distinguish four main operating models, depending on the importance assigned to high or low levels of data integration and/or process standardization. They are distinguished by four names and depicted on a two-dimensional graph.

Each operating model is adapted to a different business context. Below, we briefly describe each operating model and discuss whether it is suitable for a service-oriented approach.

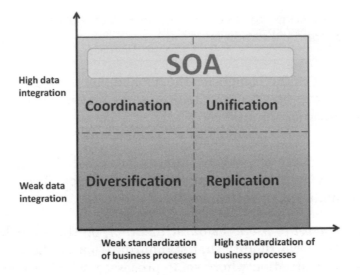

Figure A3.2. *The four operating models are defined using two axes: vertically, the degree of data integration and horizontally, the level of business-process standardization. A prerequisite for SOA to make sense is that data integration is high*

A.3.5.1. *Diversification model*

This corresponds to *weak data integration* and a *weak standardization of processes*. It is typical of companies that share few customers and few suppliers across business units. Each business unit in a company with a diversification model runs its business essentially independently from the others. Each proposes its own services to its own customers.

For these kinds of companies, innovation and independence of decision are key factors of success. They would be largely penalized if they had to comply with the semantic rigor and the discipline imposed by data integration and process standardization. Migrating to a service approach would most likely imply costs incommensurate with hypothetical benefits.

> The service approach could make sense locally, but only to couple systems living in different technological environments.

A.3.5.2. *Replication model*

This corresponds to *weak data integration* and a *high standardization of processes*.   Companies that fit this operating model leverage their ability to innovate on the global level by introducing new processes relatively quickly. Each organizational unit has a relatively large autonomy but must nevertheless comply with a large set of companywide processes. The main expected source of profit is precisely this quick, companywide implementation of new processes.

> Among the four operating models, this is probably the one that least fits a service approach.

Data integration is low to start with and increasing it would imply important costs for a goal, process flexibility, which is not needed anyway, as processes are designed in a centralized way.

A.3.5.3. *Coordination model*

In such a model, *data integration is high* but there is *no standardization of processes*. Concepts such as "customers", "suppliers", "products", "services", and "partners" are shared among the different organizational units. Some basic business processes are integrated on a global scale, but, essentially, each business unit designs its own process. The possibility of building a fully integrated customer service and the ability to track a product throughout the supply chain are the main benefits of data integration. Regarding processes, each unit can be creative. Achieving low costs is not the main concern for these companies, whose strategy is more to propose the best possible services to their customers.

> Among the four operating models, this one is no doubt the best-suited to a service approach.

The essential data, customers, products, and suppliers are already largely integrated and ready for use by each service. Moreover, the high variability of local processes fits well with the main advantage provided by a service approach.

A.3.5.4. *Unification model*

Companies that correspond to this operating model use *standardized processes based on highly integrated data*. There exists a strong coupling between the different organizational units and their autonomy is not a high priority. They strive to provide the optimized services to their customers by minimizing the variability of processes. They often use integrated supply chains, which creates strong dependences between organizational units. The management is centralized; it tries to optimize growth through economies of scale. This model is particularly well suited for companies, which sell commodities.

The fact that data is integrated allows considering a service approach. However, as most processes are designed in a centralized way:

> This operating model does not really fit into the logic of a service approach, which could nonetheless benefit, locally, to some specific processes that are not part of the core business processes.

A.3.6. Conclusion on SOA

We can identify two main reasons, which explain why many SOA projects have failed prematurely:

– Many *companies did things in the wrong order*. Rather than building a robust and scalable architecture for their stable, core processes, they tried to achieve flexibility prematurely. In the most extreme cases, this led to the so-called alignment trap, namely the IT department spending most of their energy and money on maintaining an architecture that never had the time to become mature because of premature attempts to align IT with ever-changing business requirements (see section 3.3.3). It should be emphasized that an

> SOA architecture, if useful at all, should only be considered as a last step in any enterprise-architecture maturity model. Robustness considerations should come first.

Among companies that tried to implement SOA, *many did not need it* in the first place. Companies that do not benefit from flexible business processes have no reason to switch to a service approach, as this will incur heavy financial and organizational risks for an often unpredictable outcome. Sorting the operating models according to their relevance for an SOA approach we have: (1) *replicated* (worst), (2) *diversification*, (3) *unification*, and (4) *coordination* (best suited for SOA).

It remains true, however, that, independently of any flexibility considerations, a service approach can still be partly motivated by reuse considerations, as an implementation of *simplicity through reduction* and *simplicity through organization* principles (see section 2.2).

Bibliography

[BON 11] BONNET P., *Mesure de la Valeur des Actifs Immatériels du Système d'Information*, Hermès-Lavoisier, 2011.

[CAR 03] CARR N.G., "IT doesn't matter", *Harvard Business Review*, May 2003.

[CAS 07] CASEAU Y., KROB D., PEYRONNET S., "Complexité des systèmes d'information: une famille de mesures de la complexité scalaire d'un schéma d'architecture", *Génie logiciel*, pp. 23–30, 2007.

[DEL 99] DELAHAYE J.-P., *Information, Complexité et Hasard*. Hermès-Lavoisier, 1999.

[DUG 05] DUGERDIL P., *Mesure de Complexité et Maintenance de Code*, University of Applied Sciences, Geneva, 2005.

[GIB 10] GIBON M.-N., BRONGNIART O., FALLY M., TREYER J., *Améliorer le Pilotage du SI – Le Pilotage par la Réduction de la Destruction de Valeur*, Dunod, 2010.

[GRU 04] GRUNWALD P., VITANYI P., "Shannon information and Kolmogorov complexity", *IEEE Transaction Information Theory*, http://arxiv.org/abs/cs/0410002, accessed on October 1, 2004.

[MAE 06] MAEDA J., *The Laws of Simplicity*, MIT Press, 2006.

[ROS 06] ROSS J.W., WEILL P., ROBERTSON D., *Enterprise Architecture as a Strategy – Creating a Foundation for Business Execution*, Harvard Business School Press, 2006.

[SHP 07] SHPILBERG D., BEREZ S., PURYEAR R., SHAH S., "Avoiding the alignment trap in IT", *MIT Sloan Management Review*, 2007.

[ULA 09] ULANOWICZ R.E., *A Third Window: Natural Life Beyond Newton and Darwin*, Templeton Foundation Press, 2009.

[VIR 09] VIRILIO P., *Penser la Vitesse (DVD)*, Arte Vidéo, 2009.

Index